Twayne's United States Authors Series

Sylvia E. Bowman, *Editor*

INDIANA UNIVERSITY

Louis Bromfield

LOUIS BROMFIELD

by **DAVID D. ANDERSON**

Michigan State University

 55

Twayne Publishers, Inc. :: New York

TO MY WIFE

Preface

IN THE 1920's Louis Bromfield was regarded by almost unanimous critical consensus as one of the most promising young American novelists, and in 1926 he was awarded the Pulitzer Prize. By the mid-1930's many of the same critics maintained that he had failed to realize his promise; in the background, critical disfavor manifested itself in a contempt that maintained he had succumbed to Hollywood, the book clubs, and political reaction. At his death in 1956 he was no longer taken seriously as a novelist except by his publishers, who still considered him a valuable member of their stable; by the reviewers for general journals, who praised his later novels for all the wrong reasons; and by millions of readers, to whom he gave a great deal of pleasure. By that time too he had gained a new kind of fame that was ambiguously interpreted in literary circles as that of a gentleman farmer, a practical dirt farmer, or a rural dilettante.

In such a critical climate the announcement of this first attempt to assess and evaluate Bromfield's literary works has been greeted by indifference, scepticism, and the question "Why?" There are many possible responses to each of the reactions, the most obvious of which is the fact that Bromfield was a competent writer; that many of his novels, especially the earlier works, are deserving of much more than ignominy; and that invariably his better works were uniquely American in a way that was ignored by many of his great and near-great contemporaries. To ignore these strengths because he, like so many other American writers, presumably did not live up to a hypothetical promise, is to deprive the American literary heritage of a unique, revealing interpretation of the meaning of American life.

Bromfield's view of this life belongs to a long and honorable American tradition; and it is Midwestern in its attempt to use that area as the microcosm of what had happened to the American Dream during the transformation of a wilderness into an industrial society. At the same time, Bromfield's view is peculiarly his own because he has transmuted these American characteristics into fiction by using as a basis the experiences of his own family during those years of change; by selecting, reordering, and interpreting that reality to define its meaning; and by incorporating the result in fiction that moves and lives.

The tradition that permeates Bromfield's work is Jeffersonianism with all its economic, political, and social ramifications. The closeness with which Bromfield adhered to this eighteenth-century philosophy is his most consistent characteristic; and it is, I suspect, part of the cause of the critical contempt that has been directed at his work during the past twenty years. In his early works, when he attacked materialism and industrialism for their dehumanizing effects on American life, he attacked them in Jeffersonian terms—for the very reasons that Jefferson had foreseen. At the time, these views were misinterpreted as attacks on the economic system; as such, they were considered intellectually respectable. But as he carried on in the Jeffersonian tradition by ignoring the depression-inspired demands for an economic revolution and demanded instead that America encourage its natural aristocracy, limit its government, and develop a stable, self-sufficient agricultural economy as a basis for a new world, he was considered to have lost touch with American life in the twentieth century and to have made an alliance with political and economic reaction.

Actually such was not the case. The period of the New and Fair "deals" was an era of Jacksonian democracy in which Bromfield was as uncomfortable as his mentor would have been. He had faith in his own abilities and in man in general, and he had a deep respect for human dignity. Hating the totalitarianism of fascism and communism, he feared that the Jacksonian practices of the 1930's and 1940's would lead to the same denial of human individuality in the United States; and he saw its manifestations in legally enforced equality, an emphasis upon material progress alone, and an ever-growing government. Bromfield was well aware of what was happening in America although he was unable to accept the nature of the social revolution of the 1930's; evidences of this inability in his work led to increasing polemicism, decreasing effectiveness, and critical disfavor.

Bromfield's Jeffersonian idealism manifests itself most vividly in his attempts to define the effects of industrialism and materialism on the individual human being, both in his native Midwest and in the world at large. The result he saw to be an overwhelming dehumanization that had its roots in the human characteristics of selfishness, greed, and puritanism rather than in the workings of abstract economic laws. Only a few individuals could rise above the effects of the new age, not by legislation but by natural abilities. This natural aristocracy—forever at war with the synthetic economic aristocracy—would, he hoped, eventually triumph so that it might free the masses from exploitation and economic slavery. Bromfield recognized that industrialism and its concurrent dehumanization were at the heart of the meaning of modern America, but he refused to believe that they were here to stay. Eventually, however, he came to believe that the individual, unable to escape industrialism, had to seek within its framework a new role and a new meaning for man.

Bromfield's shortcomings in interpreting the American phenomena of democracy and industrialism in the twentieth century tend to obscure the acuity with which he observed them, the faithfulness with which he recorded his impressions of their relationship to American life, and the skill with which he turned them into fiction and later into the revealing personal essays that show how closely he understood and identified himself with the Ohio countryside. It is unfortunate that this has happened.

The purpose of this study is not, however, to serve as an apology for Bromfield's shortcomings nor to reiterate that much of his work is successful. It is to examine his works as a whole in order to determine what he attempted and what he accomplished or failed to accomplish in each of them and in the canon as a whole. To do this, all of his works must be examined by use of the many tools available to the modern critic; and conclusions must be drawn from the evidence of the works rather than from the vagaries of literary and intellectual fashions, personal or literary feuds and prejudices, or the generalities of hearsay.

This book is not, of course, intended to be a biography of Bromfield, although such a study would be valuable and revealing. However, the close correlation between his life and his works makes avoidance of the facts of his life perilous, and my memories of his vigorous personality are with me as I write.

DAVID D. ANDERSON

Lansing, Michigan
December, 1962

Acknowledgments

Grateful acknowledgment is made to the following for permission to quote copyrighted material in this book:

To J. B. Lippincott Company for permission to quote from Louis Bromfield, *The Green Bay Tree* (1924), *Possession* (1925), *A Good Woman* (1927), *Twenty-Four Hours* (1930), and *A Modern Hero* (1932).

To Harper and Row, Publishers, for permission to quote from Louis Bromfield, *The Farm* (1934), *The Man Who Had Everything* (1935), *Night In Bombay* (1940), *Until the Day Break* (1942), *Out of the Earth* (1950), *Animals and Other People* (1955), and from Ellen Bromfield Geld, *The Heritage, a Daughter's Memories of Louis Bromfield* (1962).

To Random House, Inc., for permission to quote from Gertrude Stein, *The Autobiography of Alice B. Toklas* (1933).

To The Dial Press for permission to quote from Louis Bromfield in *This Is My Best*, edited by Whit Burnett (1942).

To *The Atlantic Monthly* for permission to quote from Mary Bromfield, "The Writer I Live With" (August, 1950).

To *The Nation* and *The New York Times* for permission to quote from reviews of Mr. Bromfield's works.

I am also grateful to the staffs of the Michigan State University Library, the State Library of Michigan, and the Lansing Public Library for their many courtesies; to Miss Sylvia E. Bowman for expert editorial guidance; and to Michigan State University for the All-University Research Grant Award that supported the study.

Contents

Chronology

1896　Louis Bromfield born at Mansfield, Ohio, on December 27.

1914　Graduated from high school; enrolled at Cornell to study agriculture.

1915　Withdrew from college to help run the family farm.

1916　Enrolled in Cornell in September to study journalism.

1917　Enlisted in United States Army Ambulance Service.

1917-　Served with French Army in *Section Sanitaire Américain*
1919　No. 557 as driver and interpreter. Participated in seven major battles; awarded *Croix de Guerre.*

1919　Took discharge in France; went to Paris. Returned to New York late in the year.

1920-　Worked as reporter for the New York City News Service
1922　and later as reporter and night editor for the Associated Press.

1921　Married Mary Appleton Wood on October 16.

1922-　Worked as foreign editor of *Musical America* and as
1925　assistant to producer Brock Pemberton. Was dramatic and music critic for *The Bookman,* and music critic for *Time.* Wrote a monthly column, "The New Yorker," for *The Bookman* and became advertising manager for G. P. Putnam's Sons.

1924　Published *The Green Bay Tree* on March 18. Moved to Long Island. Daughter Anne born. Began to write full time.

1925　Published *Possession* in September. Left for vacation in France.

1925-　Vacation extended to fourteen years. Leased *presbytère*
1938　in Senlis, where his daughters Hope and Ellen were born.

1926 Published *Early Autumn* in October. Awarded Pulitzer Prize.

1927 Published *A Good Woman* in July. Lectured briefly in United States.

1928 Published *The Strange Case of Miss Annie Spragg.*

1929 Published *Awake and Rehearse.*

1930 Published *Twenty-Four Hours;* worked briefly as screenwriter in Hollywood.

1932 Published *A Modern Hero;* visited India for four months that winter.

1933 Published *The Farm.* Began to talk of buying a farm in America; spent the winter in the United States.

1934 Published *Here Today and Gone Tomorrow;* wrote *De Luxe* with John Gearon and *Times Have Changed,* both produced in New York in the 1934-35 season.

1935 Published *The Man Who Had Everything,* revisited India.

1937 Published *The Rains Came.*

1938 Sent his family back to Ohio; served as president of Emergency Committee for American Wounded in Spain; returned to Ohio.

1939 Published *It Takes All Kinds;* made a *Chevalier* of the *Legion d'Honneur;* published *England, a Dying Oligarchy.* Bought three farms in Richland County, Ohio, named them "Malabar Farm," began plans for restoring the unit. Made a speaking tour, wrote briefly for Hollywood, returned to "Malabar," his home until his death.

1940 Published *Night In Bombay,* built "The Big House."

1941 Published *Wild Is the River.*

1942 Published *Until the Day Break.*

1943 Published *Mrs. Parkington.*

1944 Published *The World We Live In* and *What Became of Anna Bolton.*

1945 Published *Pleasant Valley.*

1946 Published *A Few Brass Tacks.*

1947 Published *Kenny and Colorado.*

1948 Published *The Wild Country* and *Malabar Farm.*

1950 Published *Out of the Earth;* became associated with "Malabar Farm" in Texas.

1951 Published *Mr. Smith.*

1952 Mary Wood Bromfield died in September.

1953 Became associated with *"Malabar-do-Brasil."*

1954 Published *A New Pattern for a Tired World.*

1955 Published *From My Experience* and *Animals and Other People.*

1956 Louis Bromfield died at University Hospital, Columbus, Ohio, on March 18.

CHAPTER *1*

The Formative Years

THE BACKGROUND of Louis Bromfield's work does not begin with his birth on December 27, 1896, but with the settlement of the Ohio country almost a hundred years before, when the post-Revolutionary years saw the influx of new people and new ideas into the rich land beyond the Appalachians. Two of Bromfield's great-grandfathers, Scots who had paused long enough in Maryland and Pennsylvania to absorb the temperament of the new country, made the long trip into the Ohio country in time to carve farms out of the free land; they were joined there by the third great-grandfather, a German who had come from Virginia with his wife, a member of an old Virginia family connected with the Randolphs.

These three great-grandfathers brought with them a love of the land that destroyed the virgin hardwood forests of Richland County and built a rich agricultural community that centered around Mansfield, the county seat. The site of a blockhouse in the War of 1812, Mansfield had twenty dwellings and a tavern by 1817; and it had also acquired a strange old-young transient who planted apple trees and preached the Swedenborgian doctrines of kindness, gentleness, and the imminent coming of Christ.

But the Bromfield ancestors did not absorb the romantic doctrines of Swedenborg or of any of the other sects that found their greatest appeal on the frontier. Their spiritual substance came undiluted from John Calvin and their political convictions from Thomas Jefferson; they distrusted and disliked the Baptists and Methodists who were politically Jacksonian. Hard work, thrift, sobriety, and natural ability were the tenets of their creed; and these, combined with a reverence for culture that was seemingly incongruent in a frontier society and with a distrust that bordered on contempt for the New England shopkeepers who swarmed into the area to make money from other men's sweat, were the elements of the intellectual heritage of Bromfield's parents.

As Mansfield and America changed, most abruptly in the post-Civil War years, the family doctrines remained the same. Although Bromfield's paternal grandfather was a comparative newcomer from an old New England family, the pattern had been set. The farm depressions of the 1870's and 1880's had, to a great extent, destroyed the Jeffersonian agricultural paradise that the grandparents had seen almost within reach, but they had not destroyed the dream in spite of the fact that they drove Charles Bromfield, Louis' father, off the farm to make his way in Mansfield. By 1890 the town had already become an industrial as well as a commercial center, and Charles Bromfield became in turn a store clerk, a banker, and a Democratic politician in an area that still had a strong rural Democratic bias in spite of the post-Civil War growth of Midwestern Republicanism.

In town the Bromfields belonged to the group of old families who, although unsuccessful according to the standards of the newly rich industrial and commercial families along Park Street, were nevertheless respected. In spite of his acceptance in the town, however, Charles Bromfield never lost his ties with the country. His few political successes were essentially anti-town, and his strength in the surrounding countryside lay in his love for it, his friendship with the farmers, and his dream of eventually returning to it. To further this dream, he often bought abandoned farms with the hope that he could restore them to fertility; but the ventures, in spite of faith and hard work, were all failures. Much of this dream was communicated to young Louis, however, as they traveled the countryside together on political trips and on the excursions to the abandoned farms.

From his father, Bromfield inherited, too, the Jeffersonian ideal of a pastoral society that would be perfect in the richness of its simplicity; he inherited a dislike and a distrust of industry or commerce, and of a society that deprived men of their manhood and made them bankers, bookkeepers, and factory hands. And, like his father, he believed that government, if it were allowed to, would inevitably tyrannize. This belief was reinforced for both as they saw the alliance between business and government grow in Washington and in Mansfield, while the slums multiplied in the Flats below the town and the farmers found it harder to survive.

From his mother, Bromfield inherited Scotch practicality and a firm belief in the natural aristocracy that found fulfillment in the arts as well as in close and lavish relationships with others. Annette Coulter Bromfield was determined that her children, as members of the natural aristocracy, would escape the values as well as the trades of the town and by using their abilities, ruthlessly if necessary, would achieve success in a manner that the town would respect even if it did not understand. She had a deep respect for literature that she seldom had time to read and a love of music although she was unable to play; and she was determined to find her own fulfillment as well as her children's in leading them to artistic careers. The daughter of a practical dirt farmer married to a man who would be happier on the farm, she hated what Mansfield had come to be; and even in the town, in spite of the shadow of genteel poverty that haunted her, she maintained the atmosphere of Jeffersonian plenty that she had known as a girl. As a result her home became the family gathering place for parents, brothers and sisters, cousins, and countless others. In an age that prevented the men of her family from living up to their ideals, she became a matriarch while still a young woman; and she attempted to maintain that role to the end.

Two other important family influences of these years were Louis Bromfield's two grandfathers, Thomas Bromfield and Robert Coulter, both of whom came to make their homes in the big brown house in Mansfield. Thomas Bromfield was a strange, bitter old man who as a young man had run away from his mother when she attempted to force on him her own puritan attitudes toward sex. She had attempted to force him into the ministry, and later had been responsible for the tragic suicide of Thomas' only friend. He was never reconciled with his mother; periodically he returned to Mansfield—once to marry and twice to father sons—but each time he disappeared again as though the town itself as well as its people were suffocating him. His wife struggled to rear the boys, aided by her family. Only the husband's letters from distant romantic places indicated that he was alive.

Finally, when Louis was seven, the Old Man, as he was called by the family, returned to make his home with the Bromfields and to die. Annette Bromfield accepted him as part of her burden, and for the last five years of his life he lived, bitter and alone, in a back room upstairs, where he read thick books on theology and philosophy and debated occasionally with an old crony. Thomas Bromfield was of the family but not in it; and Louis, as he carried the old man's meals to him, was alternately awed and frightened by him. Young Louis never knew but never forgot his isolated paternal grandfather.

Robert Coulter, Louis' maternal grandfather, had inherited both the family farm and a love for the soil. Long after the farm could support the numbers it once had, he remained there alone, fighting the poor agricultural economy and the decreasing fertility of the soil. Finally, old age and a bad fall from the haymow drove him from the farm. But he, unlike the old man who brooded alone upstairs, became part of the family. There was neither communication nor sympathy between the two old men; from Robert Coulter young Louis absorbed the dream that the family would some day return to the farm to live as they once had.

Their parents, grandfathers, and countless uncles, aunts, cousins, and vague connections of all sorts dominated the Bromfield children—the oldest, Marie and Louis, and Charles, the youngest—just as they were to dominate the best of Louis Bromfield's fiction. Annette Bromfield determined the means whereby each of her children was to escape the town and its values. Marie was to be a concert pianist, and before her birth a piano was bought. Her girlhood was spent at its keyboard, and she did develop into a promising young musician, but unfortunate marriages prevented fulfillment of that promise. Although she escaped the town, she died unsuccessful.

Louis and Charles were to be authors, and sets of the great nineteenth-century English novelists were procured for the boys to read as diligently as Marie practiced her music. Louis read eagerly because he enjoyed it, but Charles, who was like his father, did not possess the drive the others had inherited from their mother. Although he later attempted a career as a playwright, he gave up early and turned to business. But Louis, torn between his mother's determination to escape into the arts and his father's dream of returning to the soil, continued to read while the two natures battled in him for supremacy.

The town and the family farm combined to provide the ideal

that dominated much of Bromfield's fiction. In the town the Bromfields were considered a good family in spite of the reversal of the family fortunes and Charles's inability to "get in on" the many good things that were available for the shrewd. Mansfield had become a typical Midwestern industrial town by the beginning of the new century, and as iron and steel fabricating plants multiplied in the Flats below the town, they were surrounded by the slums that grew to house the influx of workers from central and southern Europe—men who had come to work the factories and found themselves helpless to do more than survive. At the same time, as a result of the profits from these mills, stately houses were erected on Park Street, west of the square and above and remote from the mills and the workers. Although the Bromfields lived on the right side of the square where Louis attended the good public school, and although the family attended the fashionable Congregational Church, Charles Bromfield's innate sympathy for the workers, his political activity, and his bank duties took him often into the Flats. On these journeys, as well as on those into the countryside, Louis often accompanied him, and the traditional family dislike of industrialism became hatred as he saw its effects on people. During these years, too, he learned from his schoolmates that he was poor; and his sympathy for the exploited in the Flats grew into hatred for those who made money out of tragedy.

Later, when a senior in high school, Louis worked as a newspaper reporter, seeing the brothels, the saloons, the bloody fights, and the occasional murders that made up so much of the lives of the immigrants, all of them poor and most of them ignorant and far from their women. The contrast between the clean, orderly life on the farm and the inhuman jungle that the town had become led him to think of the possibility that the dream of his father and his Grandfather Coulter might become a reality. Family finances, precarious at best, grew worse; and the family too began to think that a move back to the farm would enable them to escape the town. Annette Bromfield accepted the decision of the men in the family reluctantly because it threatened her dream for her children, but the town house was sold and in 1914 the move was made.

Bromfield, his father, and his grandfather were confident that the move would be a success and that the farm would be restored to fertility and to the financial success that it had been thirty years before. With the money from the sale of the town house, the farm buildings and fences were restored and the basis of a dairy herd purchased. But Marie had married and escaped, young Charles had no taste for farming, and Mrs. Bromfield, despite momentary enthusiasm, remained sceptical. At this point, as the money ran low and the farm was no nearer to paying its own way and to supporting the family, it was decided that Louis would go to Cornell to study scientific agriculture, an enthusiasm of all three generations of the Bromfield men.

But Bromfield's education at Cornell and his family's stay on the farm were short-lived. That fall Robert Coulter fell and broke his hip, and at the end of the first semester Bromfield returned home to help with the farm. His grandfather died, and it became increasingly evident that Annette Bromfield's scepticism about the venture was fully justified; so, playing skillfully on the dissatisfaction and the literary interests that she had implanted in her son, she encouraged his growing belief that life on the farm would lead nowhere except to hard work and oblivion. In the fall of 1916 Louis made the break that she had insisted on; he entered Columbia University to major in journalism, and he left the Richland County countryside—presumably forever.

But before the academic year was over the United States was at war. The Bromfields might have made a success of the farm during the war years, but it had been sold, and Louis was no longer interested. Instead of finishing the school year he joined a private observation balloon unit—against the strong objections of his mother—and then, in order to get overseas sooner, enlisted in the Army Ambulance Service then being organized for service with the French Army. In this unit, *Section Sanitaire Américain* No. 577, he served through seven major battles on the Western Front, receiving the *Croix de Guerre*. When his unit was to be returned to the United States in May, 1919, he took his discharge in France; he had come to know and love both the country and its people. He, like his sister Marie, had made what he felt was a final break with the town.

Early in 1919, having made up his mind that he was going to write, Louis returned to New York. With the determination of his mother, he knew exactly where he was going and how to get there. In the next few years he was successively a reporter for the New York City News Service, reporter and then night editor with Associated Press, foreign editor of *Musical America*, drama and music critic for *The Bookman,* and music critic for *Time.* He wrote a column, "The New Yorker," for *The Book-man,* became assistant to producer Brock Pemberton, and then advertising manager for G. P. Putnam's Sons. During these years he determinedly met people of all sorts, and he also found the time to court and marry Mary Appleton Wood, a socialite New Englander whose family had been transplanted to New York. At the same time he was writing novels in secret. Finishing one, he took it to Stokes, who rejected it. By 1923, as he recalled, he had written and destroyed two more, and then *The Green Bay Tree* was accepted to be published in the spring of 1924.

By the time Bromfield entered the army, the experiences and the ideas that were to provide the basis for his best novels were behind him. When he came into prominence with *The Green Bay Tree,* he had already begun to draw on them as he was to do for the following ten years. The Jeffersonian dream and the farm, both of which had dominated the family for a hundred years, continued to play a large role in his creative imagination; but they were dominated by the memory of his family, which began to take on the proportions of the characters in Dickens, Trollope, Eliot, and the others whom he had read so diligently in the brown house in Mansfield. The geography, the economics, the social structure, and the history of the town were also taking their place among the elements of his fiction. The importance of these biographical elements in the development of his work and philosophy cannot be overemphasized. In his background he recognized that he had a wealth of capital to draw on, and he was to spend it lavishly, perhaps too lavishly, in the ensuing years.

During these years, too, the forceful young man who was determined to succeed in a way that the town could never understand and to show the town that what it valued was meaningless had already begun to foreshadow the successful, wealthy author who would some day return to do those very things. After more than twenty years of fame, of fortune, and of intimacy with the greats and the would-be greats among the flashier elements of two continents, he was to return to the valley southeast of Mansfield. There, after the last of a long series of rejections of the standards and values of the twentieth century, he was to attempt a re-creation of the self-contained and fulfilling world dreamed of by his grandfather and his father. With the

energy of his nineteenth-century ancestors and the determination
of his mother, he was successful in showing the town in many
ways. He had laid bare its essential pettiness in his novels, con-
demning the values that were not his, and he came close to
success in his careers as writer and as farmer. But in both cases
success ultimately eluded his grasp.

CHAPTER 2

Defiance and Defeat

AS BROMFIELD BEGAN his writing career, determined to use as a basis the conflicts between the values of the town and those of his family, he also decided to use a simple and and very personal theme: the rejection of the town's values by the young people, of whom he was one, who fled in order to escape contamination by materialism and puritanism. The theme was simple, romantic, and timely in the years that followed World War I; and it was to contribute greatly to his early success although he, like his contemporaries, was unable to see that it was too timely and too simple to be satisfactory. Nevertheless, he used it with confidence as the basis for most of his first novel; he questioned its validity in the two immediately following, which he planned as "panel" novels, each of which was to explore another of its contemporary ramifications; and he was forced to reject it completely in the fourth.

I The Green Bay Tree

In *The Green Bay Tree* (1924) Bromfield plunges immediately into the problem of industrialism and its impact upon the individual in America between the Civil War and World War I. Ostensibly the story of Lily Shane, a beautiful, strong-willed woman who flees a Midwestern town to find peace and fulfillment in a quieter and richer existence in France, it is more precisely what Bromfield remained convinced was the story of modern civilization as it is torn between the beautiful and the practical, the ideal and the real. In the novel he depicts the ultimate triumph of the real as the ideal is trampled by brute force, by chance, and by the unpredictable vagaries of human nature itself.

The novel opens with a contrast that portrays the town, the Midwest, and the United States at the time of the Spanish-American War. In a small hedged-in park on a hill in the Flats stands a castle-like house. Festively and exotically lit for a party, its lights make it difficult to see beyond the hedge and down the hill or, in fact, to observe that the hedge itself, the trees, and the flowers and shrubs are dying, poisoned by the smoke and fumes from the factories and steel mills that surround the hill and fill the Flats.

This is the contrast that Bromfield maintains throughout the novel in setting, in values, and in people. The setting alternates at first between the house on the hill and the town itself, and then between the town and an eighteenth-century house in Paris that—for all its difference in structure, setting, and furnishings—is curiously like the house on the hill in the town. The similarity between the houses is rooted in the similarity of the women who live in them: Julia Shane in the town and her daughter Lily Shane in the house in Paris.

Julia Shane, the daughter of pioneer Scotch stock and the widow of the mysterious John Shane who had built the house at Cypress Hill when it stood isolated above the meadows and swamps of the Flats, lives there with her two daughters, Lily and Irene. Julia is contemptuous both of the mills that were eventually built around them and of the people up on the hill in town who profit by them, who whisper about her and her daughters, and who call the old place "Shane's Castle." Even while she despises the townspeople, however, she has grown wealthy through selling land to them. Nevertheless, she refuses to sell Cypress Hill to the town for a railroad station, and the controversy continues as a symbol of the old woman's proud resistance to what the town calls progress.

But, although Julia Shane knows what the inevitable outcome will be in her war with what the town has become, it is Lily's story that describes the continued fight. Proud, willful, and beautiful like her mother, at the garden party that opens the novel she deliberately seduces the bachelor governor of the state because she is drawn to him and she wants to experience sex. But the governor is part of the new alliance between business and politics that rules the state, and she refuses to marry him in spite of his pleas—just as she had refused the weak son of the

mill owner. Her younger sister, Irene, who has already rejected
the world in favor of religious asceticism, sees the governor come
from Lily's room, recognizes what has happened, and is shocked
into abhorrence of sex. But Julia Shane, when she is told, respects
Lily's decision and refuses to condemn the act.

Discovering she is pregnant, Lily goes to Paris. There she
establishes herself as a widow, secures an impoverished aristocrat to sponsor her, and gives birth to a son. Determined never
to return to the town to stay, she returns once for a visit—during
which she befriends her cousin, Ellen Tolliver, a promising
young pianist—and once at her mother's death. The house in
Paris provides the leisurely cultural existence that her father
had hoped to find in the house in the Flats before the coming
of the factories. Although Lily takes lovers, she finds fulfillment
in her freedom and refuses a series of suitors.

In the town, however, Julia Shane continues her feud with
the women who represent the new industrial aristocracy. By supporting her great nephew Charles Tolliver, the honest but inef-
fectual county treasurer, in a tax-fraud case against the political
and industrial alliance that runs the town, she secures a measure
of satisfaction, although Tolliver is defeated at the next election
and is forced to take a job in a bank. At the same time Irene
becomes active in settlement house work among the workers as
she drifts further into fanatical self-denial. Her protégé, a bright
young Ukrainian, becomes leader of the workers as they move
toward rebellion against their tormented lives, and a strike
erupts.

During the strike Julia Shane becomes ill, Lily returns, and
the old woman dies, willing the house to Lily. Irene, aiding the
strikers, is hardly conscious of her mother's death; but Lily helps
the young Ukrainian who has been wounded by the police. They
are strongly attracted to each other, and Irene, convinced that
Lily has seduced and ruined him, flees to a convent. Lily returns
to France, never to return to the ugliness and pettiness of the
town.

But the war comes, indicating to Lily that the same forces
that destroyed the town are threatening her in Europe. She is
beset by the authorities in town who want to buy Cypress Hill,
which she refuses to sell; her son Jean loses a leg in the war; and,
after a weird encounter with the first German advance, she loses

herself in relief work. Mysteriously, the old house in the town burns, and at the end of the novel she marries a French cabinet minister. She is free of the town and all that it values, but as she settles down to await her inevitable defeat, she recognizes that she is not free from the forces that made the town—and the world—what they are.

In the background, almost to the last page, Bromfield implies that Lily's escape has been successful and that she will eventually find fulfillment. Critical reviews leaped at the implication and accepted it as inevitable, but they ignored Lily's state at the end. For much earlier Bromfield begins to question as he sees the emptiness of the young people's lives:

> . . . Life is hard for our children. . . . It isn't as simple as it was for us. Their grandfathers were pioneers and the same blood runs in their veins, only they haven't a frontier any longer. They stand . . . these children of ours . . . with their backs toward this rough-hewn middle west and their faces set toward Europe and they belong to neither. They are lost somewhere between.[1]

Rebellion and personal bewilderment are there; and, in the spate of novels of personal rebellion that came from the members of the liberation groups during the 1920's, it is not surprising that *The Green Bay Tree* was included. But defiance and defeat rather than rebellion and bewilderment provide the basis of the novel. In the characters of both Julia and Lily, Bromfield emphasizes not their readiness to run but their willingness to fight for the personal freedom and integrity that they value. Even while the biological forces of old age and the economic forces of war and industrialism combine to make their defeats inevitable, each resists symbolically until resistance is futile; and each goes down to defeat as gracefully as she has lived.

It is significant that the very way of life that they both valued was actually dependent on the new age and the new values that they despised. Julia, by selling the land in the Flats for the mills, gained the wealth that made their resistance possible; Lily, by selling Cypress Hill to the town, insured that she, like her mother, could continue the tradition. Both, in a sense, triumphed over the forces of the new age by exploiting them; but each failed to realize that she had really capitulated, thereby making her defeat and the triumph of what she despised inevitable. As Lily realizes at the end of the novel, "Perhaps, after

understood his family thoroughly. But in the obviously fictitious characters of Lily's French friends, of her son, and of the workers, especially Stephen Krylenko, his portrayals are much less satisfactory. These characters are essentially puppets to be manipulated in furthering and complicating the plot.

Structurally and stylistically the novel escapes the influences of the prodigious amount of literary experimentation in the post-World War I years. Bromfield was not a member of any of the liberation movements of the time; and, in all probability, he had read very few of the "moderns"—certainly not James Joyce or Gertrude Stein. Instead the influences of Bromfield's reading of the Victorian novelists is readily apparent: the background and setting, as well as the character portrayals, are as sweeping as those of Dickens and Trollope. The solid conventionality of Bromfield's prose and the deftness with which he satirizes the representatives of the new age are qualities that would have been very much at home in the uniform sets that lined the walls of the Bromfield family library.

On the whole the novel has both strengths and weaknesses. The strength of its characterization and the forthright and rapid movement with which the story is told are among its merits, together with the sureness with which Bromfield describes the nature of the conflict between values as he describes the town. But its weaknesses are equally apparent. Foremost among them is the ambiguity with which Lily's years in France and the conclusion of the novel are handled. Bromfield is uncertain whether she has become free or has succumbed to a grimmer conformity; he prefers the former but fears the latter, thus betraying an underlying philosophical confusion that wavers between romantic idealism and pessimistic determinism. In the parts of the novel set in the town, Bromfield is sure of himself, and they are convincing; but the latter half is ultimately unsatisfactory.

Critical reception of *The Green Bay Tree* was almost uniformly good, as were its sales. Bromfield found himself established as a novelist at once, although he was sceptical of much of the praise his first book received. It was a good, craftsmanlike job, as he had intended; and it freed him to write. The royalties from the novel permitted him to quit his job at Putnam's and to move to a country house at Cold Spring Harbor, Long Island, with his wife and new daughter Anne. They were joined there by

Annette and Charles Bromfield, who had left Mansfield at Annette's insistence to follow the fortunes of their children wherever they might lead.

II Possession

Determined to follow up his first success with another, Bromfield worked furiously on *Possession,* the story of Ellen Tolliver in her rise from the town to international acclaim as a pianist. The novel was finished in the spring of 1925, and before it came out the Bromfields packed up for a brief trip to Paris—a "visit" that was to last, with brief interruptions, until the onset of World War II. In the foreword to *Possession* Bromfield defines its relationship to *The Green Bay Tree* and to the works with which he plans to follow it:

> "Possession" is in no sense a sequel to *The Green Bay Tree.* . . . The two are what might be called panel novels in a screen which, when complete, will consist of at least a half-dozen panels all interrelated and each giving a certain phase of the ungainly, swarming, glittering spectacle of American life.[3]

Paralleling in time the first novel, *Possession* contrasts—as did *The Green Bay Tree*—the restrictive life of the town and the personally liberating life abroad. But in his second novel Bromfield focuses most clearly on the effects of the respective values of those settings on his central character as she develops; he does not use setting to show the conflicting values of fully developed characters as he had earlier. As a result of these effects, the theme of the novel—while no less that of defiance and ultimate defeat than the earlier novel—is more nearly a study of the determination and the ultimate freedom that Annette Bromfield had preached to her children.

Possession opens also in the town with the portrait of a symbol of defiance, Grandpa Tolliver, ancient and indestructible, as he sits in his attic room reading *The Decline and Fall of the Roman Empire* and plotting another skirmish in his war with Hattie Tolliver, his daughter-in-law. As the old man moves through the background of the novel, without illusions, cynical, and everlastingly defiant, it becomes evident that the novel is his as much as Ellen's. He alone—the family failure and scandal—has been the only free one among them; he has been intellectually as well as physically free for a long time, and his warfare with Hattie is a means of reasserting that freedom.

In his granddaughter Ellen the old man sees the rebirth of his own determination to be free to pursue his own life without regard for others, and he is right. Ellen, oldest of the three children of Hattie and Charles Tolliver, is determined to be a rich, successful concert pianist; to do this she must study in New York and abroad, but the family finances are too precarious, and her mother's possessiveness and pride prevent her seeking help from the wealthy Shanes. To escape the town and to get to New York she elopes with Clarence Murdock, a young traveling businessman and suitor of her friend May, daughter of one of the town's industrialists.

Although Ellen has escaped the town and her mother, her marriage is impossible; she dominates the weak Clarence, and they drift apart as Ellen pursues her studies and becomes a protégé of the wealthy Therese Callendar, the matriarch of an American-European financial family. Ellen and the woman's wastrel son Richard fall in love, but Ellen refuses to divorce Clarence because she knows it will destroy him. But just when Richard marries a socialite, Clarence kills himself, revealing that he has embezzled money in order to support her. Ellen is free to go to Paris to Lily Shane, who has agreed to finance her studies.

In France she studies with the same unswerving determination, ruthlessly using the people who can help her. But, just as she begins to reach prominence as Lilli Barr, the outbreak of World War I forces her to return to America. She regards the war merely as a personal affront, but her success continues; at the end of the war she returns to Europe and acclaim. Meanwhile, her love for Richard Callendar and the machinations of his mother, old Therese, who rejects Richard's wife because she cannot produce a son, have swept her into marriage. This marriage, too, is a failure because Ellen cannot forget having been Lilli Barr and Richard cannot be faithful. A son is born, but the marriage is ended; and Ellen returns to her professional success. At the end, free of everything that had threatened to possess her, she suddenly recognizes that she is isolated and alone, just as her grandfather, now known as "The Everlasting," is alone with his books.

Although Ellen is the focal point of the novel, the story is

less hers than the story of her family and of the forces that
have come together to shape it and to tear it apart. Like *The
Green Bay Tree,* this novel is enacted against a large background
that includes many characters as well as a good deal of action.
It is not merely the story of a modern young woman who frees
herself from the forces that have enslaved women since the
beginning of civilization; it is the story of determination and
ruthlessness in a war against convention, mediocrity, and virtue.
In the end Ellen's close relationship in spirit to old Skinflint
Seton, the symbol of the town's values which she despises, is
unmistakable; and her achievement, in spite of the fact that she
is an artist, seems no more laudable. Perhaps this impression
derives from the fact that Bromfield tells that she is an artist
rather than showing it in the novel.

Although Ellen is acceptable as a person, she is not believable as an artist, a shortcoming in characterization that, while
evidently deliberate on Bromfield's part, is a serious but not
fatal flaw in the novel. Like Julia and Lily Shane in *The Green
Bay Tree,* Ellen changes almost imperceptibly as the story develops; in her determination and aloofness, her basic lack of human
feeling is present from beginning to end. Consequently, Ellen
might have become almost anything she determined to be, and
hers is not the peculiar dedication of the artist. More appropriate
perhaps would have been a career in making money at the
expense of Skinflint Seton—as her great-aunt Julia was so skillful
at doing.

Nevertheless, Bromfield effectively portrays in Ellen's character the dominant side of a characteristic that allows at best only
a stormy balance in family relations. In spite of her pity for her
first husband, her love for her second, and the sympathetic identification that we are told she feels with her brother Fergus, Ellen
is possessed of a will that almost completely obliterates human
feeling. She is effectively contrasted with her mother, Hattie
Tolliver, who, in spite of her strength, is dominated by service
to others, in return for which she demands but is unable to
secure possession. The fierce coldness of the Tolliver strain (it
is ironic that Ellen chose her maternal grandfather's name for
the stage) is incomprehensible to Hattie, just as Hattie's preoccupation with virtue and duty cannot be understood by Ellen
and "The Everlasting." In her own way, Hattie dominates the
book almost as completely as Ellen; and at the end, as Hattie

carries much of the town with her to Europe, Ellen recognizes that freedom can be futile and empty.

As in *The Green Bay Tree*, many of the lesser characters are effectively drawn. The other members of the Tolliver family—the father Charles, and the two boys, Fergus and Robert—come into clearer focus, although Bromfield disposes of all three in the course of the novel. Charles carries the Ohio countryside with him to exile and death as a tragic shadow; Fergus, the romantic, dies appropriately in an air raid on his way to a rendezvous, perhaps symbolic of Bromfield's own temporary escape from town and family; Robert, the stable, predictable one, dies ironically as a hero—thus revealing Bromfield's unresolved philosophical dilemma of this and his earlier novel. Therese Callendar is a stereotyped interpretation that goes beyond the conventional portrayal of the mysterious, willful woman of the Middle East to rival Julia Shane as a portrait of the natural aristocrat. Proud and selfish, she rises to power in the world as Julia had risen in the town. Seemingly successful and unassailable, she learns, however, that her power is limited. In her victory, she, like Bromfield's other powerful women, is defeated by circumstances, but not before she has known the power and pleasure of success.

Although Jewish characters such as Judge Weissman, the crooked politician, and Schneidermann, the industrialist-musician of *The Green Bay Tree*, persist in the background of both novels, they are stereotyped and vague, identified only by the facts that they are Jewish and that they are essentially exploiters. In *Possession*, Bromfield focuses on another, Rebecca Schönberg, Ellen's manager, in a detail that develops this stereotype and makes possible an interpretation of his own views. Rebecca, more than any other person, is responsible for the transformation of Ellen Tolliver into Lilli Barr because she has a shrewd ability to arrange appearances for their maximum promotional value and because she has an equally shrewd sense of what the public demands of the personality of a concert artist. In return for her life of service she, like Hattie Tolliver, demands an allegiance and submission that Ellen is unwilling to give. Although her role in the novel is not unlike Hattie's, and indeed the two are sometimes at odds over the disposal of Ellen's time, nevertheless Bromfield portrays her, as he does his other Jewish characters, as one who feeds on the strength of others; even old Therese

Callendar, who admits that in her, too, is a bit of Jew, is portrayed in the same vein when she displays the traits that Bromfield regards as peculiarly Jewish.

Yet this is not traditional anti-Semitism; it is a peculiarly Midwestern variety that recurs among Midwestern novelists. This attitude toward the Jew is that he is forever unknown and unknowable; of life but not in it, he stands alone, unable to break down the barriers that separate him from other men. Bromfield gives this point of view an added ironic twist of his own; his Jews do gain a measure of acceptance, but only because they can be used. Thus, while they are exploiting, they are being exploited in a way that marks them for tragedy because they, like Rebecca, know that their acceptance is a temporary convenience. Yet they can do nothing else if they are to survive in the modern world. Bromfield recognizes the problems inherent in the isolation of the Jew in the modern world; but, scarcely eight years out of the Midwest himself, he is unable as yet to explore with the perspective and clarity that this isolation demands.

In this novel, too, the women dominate; the men, with the exception of "The Everlasting," are too weak either to attempt to control their destinies or to defy the forces that manipulate them. "The Everlasting" is a curiosity from the past; he is too strong to succumb in spite of his physical helplessness, but the others have no choice. The newer generation of Charles Tolliver, Clarence Murdock, his friend Wyck, and even Richard Callendar are emasculated and destroyed because they are weak; and their destruction is wrought by the demands of their women. As Skinflint Seton observed, more wisely than he knew, in another context, "Women like that can ruin men . . . just by talking to them." [4] At the end, the strong ones—Ellen, Hattie, and Therese—carry off another manchild in triumph and expectation. "The Everlasting" reads on.

As in *The Green Bay Tree*, Bromfield is at his best when he writes of the town. As before, its physical setting is grim, its values trivial, and its way of life ruthless. But, in order to rise above its grimness and its pettiness, Bromfield sees more clearly that the same techniques must be employed to escape it as to rise in it; and Ellen, with her moments of tender intolerance that fail to reach others, is as ruthless and unscrupulous in her own way as Skinflint Seton, who loves without understanding his daughter. And while Seton's success is based on a stolen invention, Ellen's results from a stolen life.

In this case Bromfield returns to the paradox that he had portrayed in the lives of both Julia and Lily Shane. Money is the key to freedom, but at the same time it unlocks forces that in the end preclude that freedom. Just as Julia was imprisoned to wait for death in the house on the hill, isolated without final understanding, and just as Lily sat waiting in her house in Paris, so Ellen is alone at her keyboard, possessed by the music that freed her. The nature of life, Bromfield points out, is possession—among men and between men and their world. While death is an escape for the dead, even death does not free the living from the past.

Possession is considerably more complex than *The Green Bay Tree,* but the nature of its complexity makes it less satisfying. The many levels of possession with which Bromfield deals both in plot and in theme are not fully explored even in their major occurrences in his study of Ellen. But the evidence that Bromfield recognizes, even if he does not define, the complexity of his problem marks an advance over the earlier novel. The much more detailed depiction of Bromfield's own family and especially the mother-child relationship in this novel would give a Freudian analyst a great deal of joy, but more profitably it gives the novel a solid core that is lacking in its predecessor. If Ellen is ultimately unconvincing as an artist, she does live in her defiance; and Hattie and "The Everlasting" are among the most memorable characters Bromfield created. Ellen lacks the depth and stature of Julia or Lily, but as a product of the forces that clash in the Tolliver family she is a substantial character in her own right.

Both *Possession* and *The Green Bay Tree* point out the strengths and weaknesses that persist in Bromfield's fiction to the end. He can create memorable characters; he can create atmosphere and tension; he can weave them together into a fast-moving and credible plot. But his weakness—perhaps the result of the easy skill with which he wrote—is that he is unable to think through to the ultimate significances of his material: the problems of his people are neither defined nor resolved. One senses in each of these novels that the real crisis is to come; Bromfield ends on a note of triumph, but at the same time he plants the seeds of tragedy that he is unable or unwilling to let germinate.

The critical and financial success of *Possession* allowed Bromfield a freedom of choice that he had not anticipated, and his plans to return to America were abandoned. He had already begun the third of the series of novels while on Long Island in the summer of 1925, and he completed it in France as the third of his projected panel novels. The Bromfields had been living in Paris and at St. Jean de Luz on the Bay of Biscay, in both of which places Bromfield found himself a celebrity in the American and international colonies because of his first two successes. As he was taken up by this international set, Bromfield had considerably less time for sustained writing, so he began to look for a farm near Paris. Never a member of the expatriate group of American writers and artists in Paris, he had become stylish among successes in many fields and he found stimulation among a variety of people. But he did meet and form friendships with Gertrude Stein, Sinclair Lewis, Scott Fitzgerald, Edna Ferber, and a great many others, most of whom were sudden successes like himself. In spite of what had begun as a frenzied social life in France, Bromfield finished *Early Autumn* in July, 1926, and it was published that fall.

III   Early Autumn

In many ways *Early Autumn* is an abrupt change from Bromfield's first two novels. In it he has rejected the Ohio, New York, and French backgrounds of the others and has used the New England setting with which he had become acquainted through his wife; he has attempted a much more compact use of time, restricting the story to a year; and he has introduced a smaller and less varied cast of characters. In spite of these changes that indicate he was attempting a much more restrained work—perhaps in response to the few adverse criticisms that he had attempted too much to be successful in the first novels—the book is closely related to the others in theme, mood, and time. It takes its place, therefore, as the third of his panel novels.

Like the others, this novel is a story of conflict, both within the old Pentland family of Durham, Massachusetts, which is torn between adherence to the appearance and the substance of their values, and between the family and a world that no longer believes or accepts those values for which the Pentlands live. The novel is at once the acknowledgment of the possessive strength of those values and an ultimate recognition that the freedom his earlier protagonists sought with determination and found so briefly is an illusion; that one does what one must; and that the ultimate defeat that Lily Shane and Ellen Tolliver saw only as a shadow must be accepted with grace, with courage, and with the pride that comes with dignity.

The protagonist, Olivia Pentland, had married Anson Pentland, as a bewildered girl of wealthy but dubious background twenty years before. There is neither love nor respect in the marriage; it is simply one of convenience. And presumably the two, parents of a girl of eighteen and of a boy of fifteen, are destined to go to their graves after dull but impeccable lives climaxed by the publication of Anson's *The Pentland Family and the Massachusetts Bay Colony*. Olivia, the outsider, provides the strength of the family that her father-in-law, John Pentland, a strong man imprisoned by his puritan convictions, is unable to maintain as he grows older, while Anson buries himself in his research.

But the return of Sabine Callendar, a cousin who had been away for twenty years; the intrusion of a personable and successful Irish politician from Boston, Michael O'Hara; and the death of Olivia's young son Jack threaten to destroy the Pentland world. Sabine, bitter because she believes that her Pentland upbringing had made it impossible for her to hold Richard Callendar, mocks the traditions, while introducing Jean de Cyon, the son of Lily Shane, to Sybil, Olivia's daughter, and encouraging their romance. Olivia approves because she is falling in love with O'Hara, who is also aided by Sabine; she sees the possibility that both she and her daughter may escape.

But Olivia's knowledge of Anson's weakness; the death of Jack, the last of the Pentlands; and her painfully extracted promise to John Pentland that she will take care of the family fortune, heritage, and skeletons, including John's mad wife and the troublesome old Aunt Cassie, make her escape impossible. Although she encourages Sybil and Jean to elope, she sends O'Hara away to save both him and the Pentlands; and she returns to awaiting the publication of Anson's book, knowing that it is a lie and a monument to pretense. She knows that Anson and the other weak ones have no hold over her but that she can never escape the intensity with which John Pentland believes in his values. In the end she finds herself thinking as a Pentland would.

The conflicts that Bromfield portrays on almost every level of the novel resolve themselves into the basic conflict between Olivia's loyalties, a conflict that presents a dilemma: does individual strength lie in exercising the ruthlessness of an Ellen Tolliver or a Sabine Callendar, who has not learned the lesson as aptly as she might have; does it lie in the single-mindedness with which John Pentland refuses to recognize the hollowness of his values; or does it lie in the dignity with which Olivia rejects love and freedom in order to preserve the façade that hides sterile men and ideas even though she knows that appearance is a fraud? Having freed Sybil and O'Hara, Olivia doesn't permit herself to think about the nature of her decision as she returns to the mausoleum that entombs her. In the background one sees the shadow of Bromfield's other strong women.

The elopement of Sybil and Jean is the only relief in a study of defeat. And, although their roles are too minor to be of much significance, Bromfield implies that Olivia will ultimately refuse them their freedom as she finds herself thinking that Jean is a bastard and that he may adopt the Pentland name. The Pentland line, Olivia discovers had been extinguished in fact a hundred years before; an adulterous affair continued the name through John and Anson only to end it with Jack, but perhaps only temporarily if Jean sees his opportunity. Olivia and Sabine could not escape, and even cousin Horace Pentland, the remittance man, had returned in death to be buried in the family plot; there is no reason to expect that Sybil might escape any more than any of the others. In the end Olivia knows that the tradition of Pentlands and of the past will go on.

The similarities and contrasts that Bromfield employs both in character and in situations make the ultimate irony particularly effective by demonstrating the difference between appearance and reality at the same time that he shows the difficulty in distinguishing between the two. The Pentland name and tradition are more than three hundred years old, and the members of the present generation—in spite of their weakness—are by virtue of their position the heirs of both the power and the prestige as well as the responsibilities that it entails; they are aristocrats by birth. But the real aristocrats, those who are capable of accepting responsibility, are those who come out of nowhere: Olivia, to become the matriarch of future generations of Pentlands; O'Hara, to rise from poverty to political power; Jean, to give new strength to the line; and even Higgins, the groom, to provide much of the wisdom that the Pentlands lack. And yet, in spite of the strength of these people, the myth of tradition endures: O'Hara remains an upstart politician; Olivia, a slave; Jean, a potential victim; and Higgins, a stableman. Although each of them knows the truth, he can do nothing to establish it.

In the character portrayals of Aunt Cassie and Sabine and in the contrast between the funerals of young Jack and Cousin Horace, Bromfield makes use of this ultimate irony. Cassie is a caricature of the eternal virgin, the mindless meddler and gossip who is completely dominated by family mythology and by her drive to do good—and what she does is either intrinsically evil or misdirected. She had been married because girls of good station marry, but then she had taken to her bed in an illness that lasted until her bewildered husband let himself die. Then, suddenly recovered, she took over the indoctrination of orphaned Sabine, just as she later attempted to take over Olivia's. Like Anson, she wholeheartedly accepts the Pentland values without either understanding them or believing in them.

Cassie is the focal point of Sabine's bitterness because Sabine is convinced that the standards imposed on her were the cause of her inability to hold Richard Callendar, who demanded that she be a woman—something Cassie's training had forever made impossible. But Bromfield reveals that Sabine's rebellion has not freed her; her bitterness is unable to overcome the strength of Pentland tradition. In the end she is another Cassie, petty, vindictive, and enslaved, with neither the strength nor the ability to exorcise whatever it is that she senses is consuming her.

The two funerals, held a day apart in the village graveyard, are another exercise in ironic contrast. The boy's funeral is conducted by Bishop Smallwood (bitterly described by Sabine as "the Apostle to the Genteel"), who replaces the village rector to read the service from his jewel-encrusted prayer book, and the theatricality of the performance is heightened by an effort to conclude before a threatening storm breaks. The result, Sabine notes, is a hollow mockery of the fanatical Puritanism that the Pentlands had forsaken for the self-approving message of Episcopalianism. The performance, she sees, is as empty of meaning as the traditions that rule the lives of the Pentlands. The outward form of the rites is a shell, completely devoid of the belief that would give it meaning. But the boy is a Pentland, and the form must be upheld without questioning either its meaning or its value.

The funeral of Horace Pentland, who had disgraced the family and had been exiled to Europe, is secretive, furtive, and simple. Although the same Episcopal ritual is observed, it is conducted by the simple rector of the village; and the few witnesses, for there are no mourners, see the ceremony as what it is: an effort to get the family skeleton under ground and out of sight as quickly as possible. In each case the ceremony has no meaning in relationship to life, to death, or to God; it absorbs the meaning from its relationship to the tradition of the Pentlands. Even in death that tradition has its triumph because secrets are safe, and the moss-covered stones contribute to its strength.

In demonstrating the hollowness of the tradition, Bromfield uses a number of devices. As in the previous novels, whatever strength is apparent is possessed by the women. The men, who carry the Pentland name and who presumably are the protectors and extenders of the tradition, present a study in decay. John Pentland, who believes, is no longer capable of carrying on; Anson, who observes the rituals of the family, is content to live on its real and imaginary past glories although he is too weak to give them more than lip service as he distorts them to his own ends; in Jack, physical strength, too, disappears. There is no one left but the women, and the true Pentlands, the Aunt Cassies, are as devoid of strength as the men. Only new blood, that of Olivia and of Jean, can either preserve the traditions or give them meaning through belief, and Olivia's surrender insures them of both.

But it is not a new crisis, Bromfield reveals; the adulterous affair a hundred years before had insured continuation of the tradition in much the same manner, and Olivia recognizes the similarity as she discovers the truth that John Pentland had hidden because he believed in the tradition rather than the blood. His choice of Olivia as his successor is justified as she shows that she has the strength that the tradition demands; she, too, hides the truth because she knows that it would be denied or distorted by Anson and Cassie and that it would shatter the tradition.

The depth of John Pentland's belief and the strength of the tradition are revealed by the nature of his life and of his death. Since shortly after the birth of Anson, his wife has been insane; like Cassie and Sabine, she had been totally unable to accept the sexual aspect of marriage. Both she and the nature of her illness are hidden, and when it is necessary to refer to her, she is called an invalid. For almost as long John Pentland and old Mrs. Soames had been in love, and although they are so close that they look like an aging married couple to an outsider, they have never permitted any intimacies. Both of them have grown bitter as they observe the proprieties of the tradition. When Pentland is unable to stand it, he gets quietly and privately drunk and is "ill" for a few days; but the appearance and the substance of his belief are preserved. Neither Anson nor Cassie either acknowledge or understand the nature of his tragedy. In his death his belief is preserved. When it is evident that Mrs. Soames is dying, leaving him with nothing, he turns over his affairs to Olivia, abets Sybil's elopement, and then is killed in a deliberately staged riding accident. He has made his only possible escape, and his secret is safe with Olivia, Higgins, and Sabine, who by knowing and denying the truth are tied irretrievably to the tradition.

The New England aristocratic tradition is useful for Bromfield's purposes because it embodies a long-recognized standard of values and a pattern of behavior that seem in no danger of disappearing, but the novel might just as well have been set in the town of his other novels or almost anywhere else in a relatively stable society. In effect, it is the story once more of the Tolliver-Barr-Bromfield family. The oldest generation believes in the land and its values; the second generation, impotent, accepts them and the responsibilities and rituals they entail; and the third attempts to free itself from what has become meaningless, only to discover in the end that escape is impossible—as Bromfield was to discover in his own life more than ten years later. Nor is the concept a result of twentieth-century materialism, Bromfield acknowledges; the situation merely becomes intensified in a more dynamic society. A hundred years before, the adultress Savina Pentland had, in death, preserved the tradition at the same time that she brought it new blood; and even before, when Puritan settlers went out from Durham to found the town in Ohio and a new life, they also founded a new tradition, based on the old and just as rigidly observed.

The novel's New England background is less vivid than that of the town, and the novel contains some of the same weaknesses that marred the earlier two: notably a tendency to melodrama that heightens atmosphere and emotional impact at the expense of credibility, and the same propensity to ignore or avoid full exploration of the theme. Nevertheless, character, especially female, is as carefully delineated as before, and in one important way the novel marks an advance over the others. For the first time Bromfield recognizes what he had seen before only as shadow or an anticlimax to be insinuated but ignored: that is, that man does not escape. Circumstances may change, and man, if he is strong and ruthless enough, may alter the nature of his servitude; but he carries with him into any environment a predetermined psychological and environmental nature that precludes a triumph that is more than illusory and fleeting. In rejecting a conventional happy ending or even a concession to its possibility, Bromfield, in this novel, comes closer to attaining stature as an interpreter of life.

The novel indicates, too, the influence of John Galsworthy on Bromfield's work at this time. Parallels to *The Indian Summer of a Forsyte* are evident in symbol, structure, character, and even theme. On publication the novel's merits were recognized by the Pulitzer Prize for 1926, and its sales quickly surpassed those of *Possession* and *The Green Bay Tree*. Critics felt on the whole that it was further evidence that Bromfield was potentially one of the best young American novelists, although in the background skeptics pointed out that he was in too much of a hurry and that he wrote too easily to become more than a competent 'second-rater. But Bromfield, flushed with success and finding himself at home in France among the bright people who had taken him up, was at work on *A Good Woman*, which he saw as the fourth panel in the series. It was published in July, 1925.

IV A Good Woman

In the introduction to *A Good Woman*, Bromfield points out that it is the last of his panel novels, all four of which might be considered a single novel under the title *Escape*. Tied to the

others in theme, mood, and character, in it Bromfield returns
to the town as the major setting except for two sequences set in
West Africa, one at the beginning and the other at the end. In
the novel Bromfield builds on what he has learned about the
ultimate impossibility of escape in *Early Autumn* as well as on
the meaninglessness of a tradition that is accepted without belief
and that consequently becomes a force of sheer mindless destruction. The result, when combined with a much narrower scope
and a smaller range of characters, moves relentlessly to an inevitable tragedy inherent in reality and in the ironic triumph of
appearance.

Emma Downes is the "good woman." As the town sees her,
she had tragically lost her young husband years ago, but had
singlehandedly raised a young son in the path of righteousness
and had then given him to the church and to God as a missionary. At the same time she built a successful restaurant business and became a woman of property, she was prominent in the
good works of her church, and she was a leader in the suppres-
sion of vice in the community. Forty-eight as the novel opens,
she is a handsome and pure woman; her greatest pleasure is
reading her son's letters to members of her church group, and
presumably the course of her life is fixed.

But behind the appearance of goodness is the real Emma
Downes, a woman who accepts without belief. Her husband had
not died in an effort to find a fortune for his family; he had
run away from her righteousness; her religion was "a practical,
businesslike instrument of success." [5] Her son, taught to accept
the community's image of his mother, had been maneuvered
both into the mission field and into a marriage with Naomi
Potts, born and raised in the mission field and whose moment of
glory had been her girlhood reputation as "the youngest missionary of the Lord in darkest Africa." [6] Furthermore, Emma had
persuaded them that the marriage should be in name only, for
all their energies and interests must be devoted to God's work.

As the novel opens, Emma is shaken by a letter from her son
Philip announcing that the natives had attacked them, wound-
ing him slightly, and that the mission had been destroyed. More
importantly, he and Naomi are coming home; he has decided
that his calling as a missionary was a mistake. Temporarily she
is terrified; but then, remembering how well she had handled
the disappearance of her husband Jason and her son's early

ambition to be an artist, she is confident that this crisis, too, can be turned to her advantage. With prayer and skillful managing, she is sure that Philip will return to the field. In Africa, however, Philip, with the stubbornness of his mother, has seen—partly through the eyes of a proud old Englishwoman—the futility of what they are trying to do and has made up his mind. Moreover, somewhere in the savage wilderness he has caught a glimpse of beauty. Dragging with him a baffled and frightened Naomi who, unlike Emma, believes in the reality of goodness, he leaves the mission field forever.

In the town Philip resists all the machinations, pleadings, and schemes of his mother, Naomi, and his uncle, a prosperous, bigoted manufacturer. To preserve appearances, it has been announced that he has come home to recuperate; but he takes a dirty job among the foreigners in the mills. As the town begins to whisper and as Naomi finds herself helpless and confused in a hostile environment at the same time that she falls in love with her husband, both women become desperate. But Philip, attempting to find himself, begins to make friends with his co-workers and men in the town whom Emma righteously despises; and he begins to paint. Still, however, he thinks of his mother as a good woman, and he pities his wife. But the two of them conspire to regain control over him by making him a father.

Twins are born, but Philip refuses to live with Naomi. He has a recurrence of fever, participates in a strike at the mill, and pities both women but refuses to capitulate. Then, without warning, his father, Jason Downes, returns; and Emma is faced with another crisis, which is successfully interpreted to the town as a miraculous recovery of memory. Naomi, meanwhile, is moving rapidly toward tragedy. She suspects Philip of having an affair, finds circumstantial evidence to support her suspicions, and seeks comfort from the minister, whose vicious wife had made his life a hell. In their mutual torment the two run off together to escape; but their sense of hopelessness and sin overcome them, and they are found in a cheap religious boardinghouse in Pittsburgh where they had knelt down to pray and had turned on the gas.

Jason returns to Australia, dying on the way; and Emma is free to marry a congressman-admirer and she finds new opportunity for her career of righteousness. Philip, now free to marry his childhood sweetheart and to paint, is unable to escape his sense of sin in having driven Naomi to her death, and he returns to Africa to seek the beauty he had once glimpsed. There he dies of the fever, carrying with him his guilt but at last recognizing the evil his mother has done.

With this novel Bromfield has come full circle in returning to the values of the town that had driven Lily Shane and Ellen Tolliver to defiance and escape, and it provides a suitable capstone as he shows rather than tells about the mills that provide the basis of the new age. In the background Shane's Castle looms mysteriously over the Flats, Irene Shane goes unobtrusively about her business, and Lily provides a glimpse of a world that will remain forever unknown to Philip and the others. In the foreground Krylenko becomes a flesh and blood worker and human being rather than a mysterious symbol of defiance and defeat. But at the same time Bromfield's deliberate efforts to return to the situations that he had described before as contrasting background seem unnecessarily contrived, and the ensuing artificiality weakens the impact of what is otherwise a tightly constructed and well-paced plot.

This novel, more than any of the others, makes clear the futility of efforts to escape; but, it points out, one has no other choice if he is to retain his dignity and his sense of honor. In using such male characters of substance as Philip and his father Jason, Bromfield has been able for the first time to point out both the real nature of the quest and the reason for its ultimate failure. What his people seek is not freedom from values that they cannot accept, nor is it a career or a love that their environments prohibit. Rather, it is a beauty and a dignity that they have glimpsed far off and that, if attained, will give their lives meaning. In essence, Bromfield has returned, like many of his contemporaries, to the old romantic quest that had come back to dominate so much of the fiction of the 1920's in spite of the façade of realism, naturalism, and satire under which it masked. Bromfield's people, like so many others of the time, are seekers of beauty and fulfillment; but they are also lost and alone in a hostile, triumphant, and fraudulent world.

Both Philip and his father Jason illustrate clearly the nature of the quest and its ultimate end. Philip is a gentle, kind man who is incapable of the kind of flight, defiance, or ruthlessness shown by a Lily Shane or Ellen Tolliver. Instead, like Olivia, he accepts protestations of good and evil as intrinsically true, thus confusing appearance and reality and insuring his ultimate defeat in spite of his determination. But, unlike Olivia, Philip is also weak. No match for the machinations of women who are determined to have their way, he not only allows himself to be further entrapped; he makes inevitable his ultimate destruction.

Philip's father, Jason, is the most memorable male character in the panel novels, and his name symbolizes the nature of the quest of Bromfield's rebellious people. Jason is a delightful scoundrel who is completely untouched by the demands of a world that condemns him; consequently, like Jacob Barr, he is Bromfield's concept of the free man. But unlike the others, Jason has never had to fight his way out of a morass of conflicting demands; he has never permitted himself to be ensnared either by love or by bitterness; and he has never attempted to distinguish between appearance and reality. It is ironic that Emma, who condemns even the appearance of evil, finds herself lying both for herself and for him, because he, the natural man, is the only and continued love of her life. Jason has found the golden fleece that the others seek, and it has saved him; even his death is an ironic triumph over threatening old age.

But again sheer strength and determination are reserved for Bromfield's major character, Emma, who is a good woman according to all the standards of appearance that society uses to judge worth, and yet who is not a bad woman. The evil that results from her actions is neither conscious nor deliberate; instead, it is the result of her complete acceptance of those conventional standards and her determination to live up to them. Appearance to her, as to the rest of the town except for the outcasts, is the only reality. Just as Philip had accepted her in his naïveté as a good woman, in his bitterness he condemns her as evil; but he does not see that truth, lying somewhere between, is completely hidden by the two extremes. In the end, secure in her righteousness and in a position to wreak its havoc on a much larger scale, Emma, the ultimate symbol of society, is triumphant as she preaches hatred and destruction during the war.

If Emma merely accepts, Naomi believes, thus insuring her own destruction. Simple, colorless, completely naïve, Naomi believes fervently in a life of righteousness that has nothing to do with appearance and in a God who is ultimately both good

and just. Effectively contrasted with Emma, as John Pentland
is contrasted with Anson, she is the recipient of Emma's scorn,
of Philip's indifference, and of Bromfield's compassion—the first
time he has displayed it so clearly. Torn between her sense of
duty and her love for her husband, she permits love to win;
and her pathetic attempts to hold him by bearing the twins
and by futile attempts to make herself beautiful mark her as one
destined for tragedy from the beginning. The shabbiness of her
end seems to slip into melodrama, but Bromfield's compassion
keeps the emotion honest as Naomi, condemned by appearance,
finds in reality the only escape that is possible.

The background of the novel presents the most intense social
criticism of the four novels in the series. When Bromfield moves
into the Flats and the mills, he shows the same sort of compassion for its victims that he showed for Naomi, as he demonstrates that they are the victims of the same sort of forces. Caught
between the greed and self-righteousness of the people on the
hill on one hand and the uncomprehended demands of their own
natures on the other, they can only benumb themselves with
drink until, no longer able to deaden the pain, they rise up in
mindless rebellion and are smashed. The tragedy is not that of
Krylenko; he can go on to fight for dignity another day. But for
those without his strength there can be only one battle that, like
Naomi's, can have only one possible result. It is eminently fitting
that Congressman Slade, who condemns the workers in the name
of all that is virtuous and American, becomes the second husband
of Emma Downes.

In the novel, which is evidently an adaptation of the
struggle between Bromfield's grandfather, Thomas Bromfield,
and Thomas' mother, Bromfield probes into the motivating values
of those for whom the Shanes had contempt. The middle class
of the town, secure in its self-righteousness, condemns on one
hand what it sees as the godless evil of the Shanes and on the
other the brute-like evil of the foreign workers. If neither of
these classes existed, those in the middle would have had to
create them; and, in effect, this is what Bromfield has shown
that they do by re-creating them in the image of their own fears,
frustrations, and secret vices.

Although Bromfield is dealing with essentially the same problems in this novel as he had in the others, the smaller scale of
the setting and the sharpness with which the contrasts are drawn

make it more effective than the others in the panels as an expression of them. Undoubtedly this is because in returning to the town Bromfield is on firm ground, just as he had been in the first parts of *The Green Bay Tree* and *Possession*. But his consistent setting in this novel, except for the African scenes that provide contrast and framing, prevents the almost physical break that occurs in the first two. The result is a believable intensity that the others lack.

In spite of its intensity the novel is marred by a number of shortcomings, the most serious of which lies in the portrayal of Philip. In spite of the detail with which Bromfield has described the closeness of the relationship between mother and son—even in such incidents as his boyhood memories of his tired mother bending over a hot oven or scheming to make a Christmas, visions that rise to blot out his suspicions—Philip never becomes quite believable. With the intelligence with which he is accredited, one would expect him to move through the pages with more life than a shadow. His characterization does, however, further document the fact that Bromfield's real strength lies in portraying female characters.

Two other outstanding weaknesses detract from the ultimate effectiveness of the book. One is the obviousness with which Bromfield contrives to introduce the characters of *The Green Bay Tree* into the story, a factor that actually adds nothing because they are unimportant as people to the operation of plot or motivation. The other weakness is the sustained image of the town as an anthill, an image that is both hackneyed and inappropriate.

With the conclusion of *A Good Woman* as the last panel in his series of novels, Bromfield not only had gained a large measure of critical approval, if not acclaim; but he had also accomplished a substantial amount of good and promising work. With a seemingly inexhaustible background of material to draw from, the ability to construct believable characters in an intense situation, and a talent for writing both rapidly and well—all of which he displayed in his first four novels—it was evident that his shortcomings were of the sort that could be removed by experience and by closer attention to the details that make up the art of fiction. Critical consensus placed him rightfully among the most promising of his contemporary young novelists.

In his accomplishment he was very much a man of the time;

if less daring than Fitzgerald, he was no less eager to explore the nature and meaning of a suddenly affluent and aimless society; and, like so many of the others, he strained at the ties of a world devoted to things. In doing so, like his contemporaries Ernest Hemingway, Sherwood Anderson, Eugene O'Neill, and others, he had taken up a romantic quest for meaning by carrying out and portraying in his fiction a rebellion and an exposure of shortcomings that—to the artist of the 1920's, who sneered at the term romantic—was harshly realistic. But the very nature of the new world that they sought made it unattainable, and the only meaning they found was in the act of rebellion itself. As Bromfield recognized much earlier than the others, rebellion, undertaken in confidence and with determination, leads to ultimate defeat.

Although Bromfield did not know it at the time, with the conclusion of *A Good Woman* he had ended one phase of his literary career and had started another. The shift may be ascribed to many things, perhaps to a reluctance to use any more of the family material, a desire to seek new subject matter in the material that he had gathered in New York and France, or a response to the demands of critics, publisher, and public not only to maintain his pace but to give them something new. Whatever the reason, at this point Bromfield put the panel novels that had their origin in his own Midwestern background behind him, although he was to draw on that material in *The Strange Case of Miss Annie Spragg,* on which he was already at work.

CHAPTER 3

The Years of Irresolution

DURING THE YEARS that Bromfield wrote his first four novels, he had been doing other things in spite of the intensity with which he wrote. In response to demands for his appearance, he gave informal lectures in both the United States and France; he wrote short stories for both popular and serious magazines; and he was asked to contribute chapters to several collective works. The first of these collective works was a novel called *Bobbed Hair,* a light-hearted spoof of contemporary romantic novels to which each of twenty Americans contributed a chapter designed to satirize the spirit of the 1920's. Bromfield's chapter intensifies the atmosphere of fun and also satirizes the determinedly symbolic devices in such novels that demand attention to themselves at the expense of credibility and artistic unity.

Among the other contributions to collective works are the chapters "Expatriate—Vintage 1927" in *Mirrors of the Year, 1926-1927,* "A Critique of Criticism" in *Revolt in the Arts,* and "Hawthorne" in *The Writers of American Literature.* The three essays are directly related to Bromfield's activities at the time; and, from the vantage point provided by his acknowledged position as a promising young writer, he made a number of observations typical of the definitive pronouncements to which young writers are addicted. In "Expatriate—Vintage 1927" he asserts that there is no longer such a phenomenon as the expatriate of Henry James's day; instead America, no longer the country of unsophisticates, has come of age and has exported its culture to Europe. Hence, Americans in Europe are free in a sense impossible to James's people, free either to pose or to produce and at the same time able to understand America.

In "A Critique of Criticism" he asserts that book reviewing has vanished, to be replaced by a mad critical search for "best" books that produces fantastic pronouncements, wisecracking, and critical exhibitionism at the expense of much that is worthy of careful attention. In "The Novel in Transition" he builds on this idea by denying that there is anything approaching a revolt in the novel; rather he sees a logical development approaching frankness in treatment of material and the use of new techniques in character development in response to artistic demands rather than as a result of the iconoclasm inherent in a conscious revolt. "Hawthorne" is simply a sympathetic, mature appraisal of the loneliness of the artist in America as reflected in Hawthorne's work.

In late 1927 Bromfield gave a series of lectures in the United States under the sponsorship of the Leigh-Emmerick Lecture Bureau. A commercial enterprise designed to capitalize on his growing reputation, it was distasteful to him. As soon as his contract was completed, he returned to France.

During these years, too, the pattern of Bromfield's life abroad as it was to be until the outbreak of World War II was largely set. As popular members of the international set in the flush years before the crash of 1929, he and Mary Bromfield came to know the kinds of people who most interested him—writers, actors, exiled nobility, businessmen, remittance men, impoverished "nice" ladies, and the hangers-on that inevitably are attracted to such gatherings. It was a mixed group, as Mary Bromfield later described it with a faint touch of New England disapproval and with no indication of her own interests and preferences: "He prefers to be with those who entertain and interest him, rather than with those who could advance him." [1]

Typical of Bromfield's encounters during these years was the beginning of his friendship with Gertrude Stein. As she describes it,

> One day Gertrude Stein came home from a walk to the bank and bringing out a card from her pocket said, we are lunching tomorrow with the Bromfields. Way back in the Hemingway days Gertrude Stein had met Bromfield and his wife and then from time to time there had been a slight acquaintance, there had even been a slight acquaintance with Bromfield's sister, and now suddenly we were lunching with the Bromfields. Why, I asked, because answered Gertrude Stein quite radiant, he knows all about gardens.
>
> We lunched with the Bromfields and he does know all about

gardens and all about flowers and all about soils. Gertrude Stein
and he first liked each other as gardeners, then they liked each
other as americans and then they liked each other as writers.
Gertrude Stein says of him that he is as american as Jane
Scudder, as american as a doughboy, but not as solemn.[2]

As a base of operations for the rest of his stay in France,
Bromfield had taken a fifty-year lease on an old *Presbytère* in
the village of Senlis, thirty-five miles north of Paris. Once the
home of Capuchin monks, it had several acres of land, including
a large garden which its previous occupants had made from a
medieval graveyard. Along one side ran the Nonnette River, and
at the end stood a thirteenth-century chapel, long abandoned,
which Bromfield made into a sort of greenhouse. Most of his idle
moments were spent working in the garden, and here in France
his other two daughters were born: Hope in 1929, and Ellen in
1932. As a place close to the soil at which he could entertain
his friends and as a base for excursions to Italy, to Switzerland,
and even back to America, it was ideal, as Ellen Bromfield Geld
recalls in her memoir. Here, after an Italian journey, he wrote
The Strange Case of Miss Annie Spragg.

I   The Strange Case of Miss Annie Spragg

This novel is a radical departure from Bromfield's earlier work
in setting, structure, theme, and characterization. The setting is
the small Italian town of Brinoë, a haven for British and American expatriates, most of them genteelly poor and all of them
leading lives of quiet desperation. Although "the season" is over,
the principal characters remain in town for various reasons; and
the revelations that follow the death of Miss Annie Spragg provide Bromfield with the opportunity to explore the background
and the nature of the characters in detail. The device is an old
one that had won the Pulitzer Prize for Thornton Wilder's *The
Bridge of San Luis Rey* the year before, but Bromfield brings
originality to it as he defines the strange combination of sensuousness and mysticism that ties the characters together. Lacking
a definite plot structure, the novel ranges widely in its search
for origins and relationships that cause and stem from the strange
death and apparently miraculous life of Miss Annie Spragg.
The novel opens and closes with the observations of Mr.

Winnery, a middle-aged English gentleman who lives on a pittance from an elderly uncle and on what he can earn from a second-hand gossip column in a woman's magazine. A former contributor to *The Yellow Book* and an intimate of Oscar Wilde and others, he finds himself living not only for the death of his young aunt so that he may inherit the family fortune but for the publication of his definitive study, *Miracles and Other Natural Phenomena.* In the process of explaining the natural phenomenon of Annie Spragg, the gentle cynic meets Mrs. Weatherby, a rich American lady who has devoted her life to stylish mysticism; the worldly and faithless Father d'Astier, in whose nature the spirit and the flesh war ceaselessly; the aging and passionate Principessa d'Orobelli who pursues love and youth, but regrets that her love for Father d'Astier has never been consummated; and Miss Fosdick, Mrs. Weatherby's poor companion, with whom Mr. Winnery finds love. In the process, too, he unfolds the story of Annie Spragg and he provides opportunity for the introduction of his aunt, Bessie Cudlip, and for the story of the mysterious line of Spraggs who culminated in the miracle of Annie.

As the novel opens Miss Annie Spragg, a poor American spinster, is dead. As Sister Annunziata, who serves the poor (and who is also the sister-in-law of the Principessa d'Orobelli), and Father Baldessare, a stupid but devout young priest (who is the illegitimate son of Father d'Astier), prepare her for burial, it is noted that wild birds fly fearlessly around her room and that she is marked by the stigmata. Sister Annunziata sees a vision that has personal significance for her, and the poor of the town believe that a miracle has been performed and that Annie is a saint. The Church withholds comment, and Mr. Winnery seeks his natural explanation, only to find a mysterious sequence of relationships that range from pre-Christian deities to a primitive frontier religious sect in the nineteenth-century American Midwest.

In his portrayal of Annie's background among the Spraggites and Primitive Methodists in the Midwest, Bromfield is on the surest ground in the novel. Such sects as the Spraggites, essentially Perfectionists who were known as free-lovers among nonbelievers, were almost commonplace on the American frontier; there were several within a fifty-mile radius of Mansfield at various times during the nineteenth century. Cyrus Spragg, Annie's father, wanders through the frontier, preaching damna-

tion and seducing women, until he and his followers erect a New
Jerusalem, a cooperative commonwealth, and a temple dedicated
to God and to Spragg's special devotions with the temple virgins.
But the colony disintegrates in scandal at Spragg's death, and
his son Uriah goes off to expiate his father's sin as a Primitive
Methodist, taking the sensuous but frightened Annie with him.

Tragedy and death follow them. Leander Potts, a divinity stu-
dent who loves Annie, kills himself, and Annie and Uriah are
driven from town to town, while Uriah attempts to drive what he
sees as the lust of the flesh out of Annie by a series of physical
and psychological tortures. Finally, just as they are about to
be driven from the only parish that had accepted them, Uriah
is mysteriously murdered, and Annie goes to Brinoë to live.

In the background, both in America and in Italy, there are
stories about Annie that include her mysterious relationship with
animals, especially birds and male goats, with which she is
reported to dance naked in the moonlight; there are unexplained
violent deaths; there is the demented Irish boy in Iowa who dies
at the same hour that Annie dies in Italy; there is the remarkable
coincidence in which a statue of the ancient fertility god Priapus
that was excavated in Mrs. Weatherby's garden is discovered to
be the exact image of an old tintype of Cyrus Spragg; there is
the use of Annie's bed as a fertility omen by a practitioner of
black magic in the village. Mr. Winnery marshals the evidence
for and against a natural explanation of Annie's existence, but
as the novel closes he loses interest. Affluent, married to Miss
Fosdick, and established in the villa where Priapus had been
discovered, he and his wife have begun to raise a family. Perhaps, he concludes, there are other than natural phenomena.

The other characters in the novel display none of the remarkable fertility of Mr. Winnery and Miss Fosdick, but each finds
peace of a sort: the Principessa with a young Italian count,
Father d'Astier in the old age that allows him to win his battle,
Sister Annunziata in madness that lets her forget, and Father
Baldessare in death at the hands of a mob as he seeks to purify
the Church. Bessie Cudlip, Winnery's aunt, maintains her peace
in a life of service and innate dignity.

The Strange Case of Miss Annie Spragg, like Bromfield's earlier
novels, is a study in contrasts, out of which he draws his theme.
At its core is a contrast between the simple and the sophisticated.
It is most obvious in the difference between a London pub and

a continental salon, but the same contrast is shown in character portrayals and in religious differences. Ultimately, however, Bromfield proclaims that the apparent contrasts are in appearance only, that the real conflicts are internal, and that only the resolution of them brings any sort of peace. But resolution through the intellect is both useless and unimportant; it can only come with acceptance and belief, as Olivia Pentland had already learned in *Early Autumn*.

The contrasts between Bessie Cudlip and the Principessa d'Orobelli, and between Cyrus Spragg and Father d'Astier, provide the basis for Bromfield's statement. Bessie is a barmaid, a big girl with a heart as big as her expansive nature; and she gives freely of everything she has to give, from herself in her youth to the money she inherits in her premature middle age. Bessie accepts life and she intuitively believes in it, as the more sophisticated—who probe it, run from it, and attempt to deny it— cannot do; consequently, she finds the meaning and fulfillment that elude the others. In her simple-minded acceptance she is the reverse of Emma Downes; she is naturally a good woman in whom Bromfield has drawn, with Dickensian sharpness and whimsicality, a character who is unique among all of Bromfield's women. She is more natural, more humorous, more human, and hence more appealing than the determined, forceful women he had portrayed in the earlier novels.

The Principessa d'Orobelli is Bessie's complete opposite. In her regret for the lost love of her youth and in her determined efforts to recapture it, she devotes herself to the diet, cosmetics, and exercise necessary to maintain her appearance and to the pursuit of a series of much younger lovers. Whereas Bessie accepts life as it is as both natural and good, the Principessa is looking for a permanence and fulfillment that it does not contain. The resulting fears and frustrations lead her to a life that precludes peace and fulfillment, as it makes of her a mask behind which is seen the ultimate horror that comes from fear.

In the figures of Cyrus Spragg and Father d'Astier Bromfield contrasts two opposing interpretations of the nature of life, a phenomenon that is ultimately unexplainable. Both Spragg and d'Astier are made of that combination of mysticism and sensuousness that so often seeks expression in religion and that frequently results in a tragic inability to reconcile the two. Spragg, crude, forceful, and dynamic, eventually permits the sensuous side to predominate, and the result is reaction and horror. Father d'Astier is witty, urbane, and civilized, yet he is torn by the same sort of forces. Unlike Spragg, he denies the flesh; but the result is the same as he destroys the faith of his son and permits the Principessa to go on to her own private hell while he waits for the ultimate answer that he is not sure exists.

At the heart of these characterizations is Bromfield's view of the apparent dichotomy between flesh and spirit that man has tried to resolve throughout his history, a dichotomy that the novel denies exists. Man's ultimate concern in every religion from the most primitive to the most sophisticated is not the nature and meaning of God as a being apart, but is the nature and meaning of life itself, the only manifestation of God that man can know. But each man, in denying this ultimate truth, or in distorting it to serve ends other than life itself, obscures the truth and in so doing denies the fulfillment that life can offer. In many ways the novel is not only an answer to the problems faced by Annie Spragg and the others but also an explanation of the irony implicit in Emma Downes and the tragic guilt of her son. Peace and fulfillment can be found, but only the Bessie Cudlips, who intuitively perceive it, and the Mr. Winnerys, who regard life in its natural aspects, are permitted to find it.

The peculiar structure of the novel contributes both to its effectiveness and to the adverse criticism that has been leveled against it. In contrast to the continuous chronological narratives of the earlier novels, this book is actually a series of integrated stories that, through their collective contributions to the theme and the exposition of the situation in Brinoë, approximate the novel form. As a result, the intensity and effectiveness of the whole suffers from the often arbitrary insertion of stories; but at the same time Bromfield has done a remarkable job of recreating Annie Spragg, who is never a human being but only an extension of others as they interpret her according to their own beliefs and superstitions.

The novel is weakened both by Bromfield's arbitrary insertion of material that can only be learned by Winnery much later than the time sequence of the novel allows and by the insertion of material, notably the story of Bessie Cudlip, that seems irrelevant to the Annie Spragg story, although both are related through theme and motivation. This factor makes the book more nearly a series of closely related short stories than a novel. As a result the same sense of deliberate contrivance that marred *A Good Woman* is present.

At the same time the book exhibits both an intensity that results from concentration and an ambiguity deliberately designed to open up areas of interpretation that are new in Bromfield's work. But underneath the ambiguity it is evident that Bromfield has fully committed himself to belief in a natural life that accepts the imponderability of the forces that are manifested by both the physical and the spiritual worlds. While he admits that man knows nothing of his ultimate nature, nevertheless he asserts that the two worlds are one.

Although a case may be made for the interpretation of Mr. Winnery as a projection of Bromfield himself because Bromfield gave Winnery much of his own scepticism and used some observations that came from his Ohio background, the emphasis on such a relationship is tenuous at best. This is the first of Bromfield's books in which his background plays almost no part, and the new material that he had been gathering from the people whom he had observed in Europe becomes proportionately more important. This direction was to provide greater flexibility in his later work.

This novel, too, was generally well received, although a number of critics observed that it marked no real advance over his previous work as, indeed, in spite of its departure from his earlier techniques, it did not. Nevertheless, it contributed to furthering his popularity, and shortly after it appeared, Samuel Goldwyn offered him an extended contract as a screenwriter at $2,500 a week. Bromfield accepted. After a frustrating year during which he accomplished little except the preparation of a volume of previously written short stories, he paid Goldwyn $10,000 to be released from his contract so that he could return to the *Presbytère*, his garden, and writing.

The Hollywood fiasco did, however, influence the course of Bromfield's future work in another way. It introduced him to George Hawkins, the sort of colorful hanger-on who is often found on the periphery of show business. Assigned by Goldwyn to help Bromfield with his paper work, Hawkins remained with Bromfield as manager-secretary as well as jovial member of the household until his death almost twenty years later. Hawkins had a story sense that, according to Ellen Bromfield Geld, was often, through argument, cajolery, or even reason, influential in determining the nature of Bromfield's works during those years. At the same time, unfortunately, he knew the demands of show business. Mrs. Geld describes such typical incidents:

> He could thrust a manuscript under the Boss's nose and roar with the indignation of an enraged bull, "You don't mean to sit there and tell me to type *this* crap! I never read such uninhibited corn in my life!"
>
> And yet, in another moment, I can hear him say in a matter-of-fact tone all the more touching for its marked carelessness, "You know, Lou, that stuff you handed me this morning is damned good. Goldwyn would sink a pile into that. If I were you, I wouldn't change a thing." [3]

The total effect of Hawkins' influence on Bromfield's future work is, of course, impossible to determine; but Mrs. Geld feels that, with his instinct for a story, it was ultimately good. Certainly its strength is attested to by a ridiculous rumor, still current in the Mansfield area, that Hawkins actually wrote many of Bromfield's later novels. It is, however, evident that shortly after Bromfield's abortive affair with Hollywood, a change gradually began to appear in his novels. At the same time that the intense air of conviction began to disappear, a lack of reality began to emerge. With the major exceptions of *The Farm* and *The Rains Came* Bromfield began to reserve much of his conviction for his nonfiction.

II Awake and Rehearse

While Bromfield was engaged in fulfilling his Hollywood contract by occasional appearances at his office and by a good deal of partying, his next book, *Awake and Rehearse,* appeared in 1929. The book was a mistake, and it did lasting damage to Bromfield's reputation with the critics because it permitted those who had doubted his abilities or his integrity to become more vocal. Its appearance marks the beginning of the accusation of commercialism that influenced the judgment of much later good work.

Awake and Rehearse is a collection of almost uniformly weak or mediocre stories that were written for popular magazines during the 1920's. Most of them had been published in such magazines as *McCall's, Harper's Bazaar, Collier's* and others, but some had evidently been rejected or perhaps newly written for the collection. In spite of their occasional individual merits, they do provide evidence that Bromfield's real talents were not for the short story.

In the best of the stories, "The Life of Vergie Winters," Bromfield returns to the town to describe, with a good deal of compassion and not a little irony, a lifetime affair between Vergie, a poor but proud milliner, and John Shadwell, a politician who becomes a political power. Although they are discreet, rumors are heard; and, in accordance with the peculiar double standard of American puritanism, Vergie is ostracized while Shadwell's career advances. Although Vergie is forced to give up her daughter to adoption and to the town's standards, she is secure in her love; and in the end she knows that she has had her love fulfilled in a way that very few people do. Finally, however, even the memory of the scandal is lost to the town, and only an old monument to Shadwell in the square is left as an indication that the lovers had ever lived.

In this story, as in the background of the novels, Bromfield displays his insight into the mores and values of late nineteenth-century America as successfully as it can be done; he is repulsed by those standards but at the same time he reveals an air of nostalgia at the passing of the closeness that they represent. But he does not condemn either the standards or the people who enforce them, nor does he descend to sentimentality; his compassion for Vergie and his pride in her strength and courage allow him only regret. Vergie takes her place in the array of Bromfield's great women characters; Shadwell, who leans on her strength, is one of his typical men.

This story shows its superiority to the others in the collection in another way: this is a story in which Bromfield believes, and this sincerity gives it an air of strength and conviction that the others lack. Only in "The Life of Zenobia White" did he attempt the same thing, with much less success, as he recognized; he was to return to its subject matter in more effective future works. "The Apothecary," too, is a sound story, dealing with the decadent international set of discredited and impoverished nobility, the new-rich who are attempting to trade money for prestige, and the complete innocence of the young American girl whom the others attempt to exploit through the agency of an American woman of dubious background who serves them. In the background the apothecary in life and his stench after death reveal the situation for what it is. Bromfield had tried to use this theme earlier in "The Cat Who Lived at the Ritz," but in that story an air of phony sophistication resulting from its weak point of view and irrelevant symbolism made it ineffective.

"Justice," too, is more effective than the bulk of the stories. Written in 1925 when Bromfield was reading Galsworthy, it is the story of a man who is convicted by society and by the weakness of the narrator rather than by the evidence. The intensity of "The Apothecary" and the depth of "The Life of Vergie Winters" are, however, lacking, and the closeness of its theme to Galsworthy's play reveals that it is an exercise rather than a serious attempt. Nevertheless, it does point out the debt, both thematically and structurally, that Bromfield's earlier works owe to Galsworthy—a point noted by a number of his reviewers, both in praise and in condemnation.

The other stories in the collection are hardly worth critical attention. Although each of them has its own peculiar weaknesses, shortcomings common to them all are their superficiality and obviousness. At the same time, in searching for verisimilitude, Bromfield has often indulged in triteness; and the result is a slick lack of conviction on the part of either Bromfield or his reader.

There are evidences that Bromfield regarded most of these stories as exercises or tentative explorations of theme and situation rather than as final works. The stories are centered around deaths and funerals and the resulting influences on the living. The repetitive nature of the stories, including the re-use of a boxful of human ashes, indicates their experimental nature. Nevertheless, regardless of pressures from publisher or public, Bromfield should not have permitted the collection to appear; the few good stories could have waited for a more selective collection; the others, like the commercial stories of Scott Fitzgerald, are best forgotten.

III   Twenty-Four Hours

Bromfield's next novel, *Twenty-Four Hours*, was published in the summer of 1930, shortly after he broke his screen-writing contract with Samuel Goldwyn. Begun in 1925, probably as one of the panel novels, as several early references show; then put aside in favor of *Early Autumn;* revived after *The Strange Case of Miss Annie Spragg;* and worked on sporadically until it was finished in August, 1929, but not published until a year later, it marks a decline from the achievements of the earlier novels. And it is evident that Bromfield was aware of this, although, like *Awake and Rehearse,* he allowed the book to be published. This novel, however, unlike most of the stories in the collection, is not a bad novel; it is merely weak in execution and structure. The characterization remains strong, and it might have been a good book had Bromfield developed his theme logically. Nevertheless, from the point of view of Bromfield's ideological development, it is extremely important. Perhaps his difficulty in articulating its basic philosophic premise accounts for the trouble he had writing it.

The novel takes place during the twenty-four-hour period of a winter day in New York of the 1920's. Within this period Bromfield attempts to portray every level of the city's life, from violent crime to high finance and from the cheap waterfront hotels along the North River to the mansions of Murray Hill—all tied together through a series of dramatic character and situation sketches. Such an ambitious scheme called for careful execution; perhaps ambition, as well as its ultimately unsatisfactory execution, is responsible for the book's failure in spite of its strengths.

The novel opens with a dinner party given by aging Hector Champion, an effeminate and frightened old aristocrat; and it closes with a tea given the next afternoon by Savina Jerrald, also an aging aristocrat but one possessed of the strength that should have been Hector's. At the dinner is a cross-section of New York society of the 1920's, ranging from the wealthy and aristocratic but weak Fanny and Jim Towner through David Melbourn and Mrs. Wintringham, both of whom have risen by their own determination, to young Philip Dantry, Hector's nephew. Son of a strong, common father, Philip has inherited his father's looks but not his strength.

During the next twenty-four hours each of them meets and resolves a crisis in his life, with the exception of old Hector, who must have his resolved for him. Philip blindly allows himself to be married by a scheming, momentarily fashionable actress; Melbourn breaks off his affair with Mrs. Towner and finds love with Mrs. Wintringham; Towner, after escaping the scandal of the sordid murder of his mistress, is reconciled with his wife; and Savina determines to marry old Hector, whom she has loved for years, in order to save him from himself.

In tying all these stories and ends together, Bromfield depends on characterization, coincidence, and sometimes sheer trickery; but the remarkable point is that he almost brings it off. If characterization, his strong point in earlier novels, had not slipped at times and if he had dispensed with trickery, perhaps by extending the time or by attempting a less tight relationship, he might have succeeded by focusing clearly on the ultimate tragedy that the novel implies.

In spite of its ultimate weakness there are many elements in the novel that relate it to Bromfield's earlier work—for the most part elements of strength. Too, there are indications of the direction that his future work is to take, and there is one feature that marks an advance over his earlier work: the characterization of David Melbourn, Bromfield's first major male character who is both strong and well defined. One of the most sympathetic characters in the novel, Melbourn is another example of Bromfield's concept of the natural aristocrat. Out of a Midwestern background very much like Bromfield's own, Melbourn works his way up, through dedication, determination, and more than a touch of sharp dealing (which is justified because "everybody did it in those days"),[4] to a position of power as one of the wealthiest men in the country. In the process he has acquired a strength and a sense of human values that the old hereditary aristocrat, Hector Champion, cannot understand.

In keeping with Melbourn's strong belief in the individualism that makes possible the rise of people such as himself, he rejects the increasingly stylish socialism because he feels that most of the poor could, like himself, rise out of that world if they had the will and the fortitude. He admits he is a poor democrat in the Jacksonian sense of the word, but such democracy has no place in his standard of values. He has a strong sense of the herd that surrounds him, but he recognizes that he is above them. Moreover, he seeks a woman who is strong enough yet feminine enough to share that high place with him. Presented as unscrupulous but as not wrongly so, he is a sympathetic as well as strong portrayal of the truly self-made man, a portrayal that contrasts sharply with the social consciousness of the earlier novels. At the same time Melbourn's unconscious smugness, a characteristic that Bromfield may or may not have intended to convey, precludes any sense of warmth toward or identification with him.

As in the earlier novels, Bromfield sets up contrasts, and Melbourn is contrasted effectively with Hector, Jim Towner, and Philip Dantry—all members of the hereditary aristocracy, all weak, all goalless, and all born to be emasculated by unscrupulous women. Hector had been destroyed by his mother and sister; Towner, by his wife; and Dantry, weakened by his environment, is to be destroyed by his actress wife, Janie Fagan. Although membership in the hereditary aristocracy does not preclude membership in the natural aristocracy, the very characteristics that determine the natural aristocrat are those that are necessary to the struggle to rise—strength, intelligence, and a standard of values based on reality rather than on appearance; these characteristics are inhibited or denied by the environment that produces the hereditary aristocrat. Consequently, membership in both classes is unlikely.

Savina Jerrald, like others of Bromfield's women, is one of those unlikely examples. Another of Bromfield's strong women, she has in all the significant aspects of her life rejected the values of Hector Champion for a strong sense of reality and an ability to base judgments on realistic appraisals of worth rather than on the standards of her class, especially in the perception of human values. She has known for most of her life what she wants out of life, and in the course of the twenty-four hours of the story's duration she finally sees it within her grasp. But Savina is the only one of the hereditary aristocracy, male or female, who is also a member of the natural aristocracy; Fanny Towner, on the other hand, is weak and vacillating. Never knowing what she wants, she is unable to secure it; in the end her reconciliation with her husband is a temporary expedient that, like young Dantry's marriage, has overtones of tragedy.

Savina's counterpart among the women is Mrs. Wintringham, a complete woman who has become an adventuress through necessity. Strong, rational, and determined, yet possessed of the sense of natural values and intrinsic worth that marks the natural aristocrat, she, like Melbourn, has made a secure place for herself in a hostile world. It is significant that the only people in the novel who intuitively recognize her worth are

Savina and Melbourn. Savina accepts Mrs. Wintringham in preference to women of her own class, while Melbourn rejects the soulless froth of his mistress, Fanny Towner, so that he may marry Mrs. Wintringham. Their mutual strengths, appropriate for each of their sexes, and their mutual grasp on reality will provide the fulfillment the others never find.

At the same time, on the lower levels of society Bromfield also provides contrasts with his natural aristocracy. The doormen and streetcar conductors are what they are, not because they are evil or weak, but simply because they don't have the strength, dedication, and intelligence to seek to better themselves. Janie Fagan attains a modicum of popular acceptance, but her inability to perceive the difference between reality and her world of make-believe keeps her forever cheap, as Savina recognizes; and Rosa Dugan, Towner's mistress, is murdered because she lacks the ruthlessness necessary to say no to those who need her. These shortcomings are in the natures of the people themselves; hence, these individuals are naturally part of the herd and are doomed by heredity to monotony, frustration, and tragedy, just as the same shortcomings prevent members of the hereditary aristocracy from attaining the fulfillment that people like Melbourn seek and find.

In the novel, too, Bromfield comes close to defining the essential factor that determines membership in his natural aristocracy at the same time that he advances a tentative resolution of the apparent dichotomy in *The Strange Case of Miss Annie Spragg*. This is a recognition, pointed out by both Savina and Mrs. Wintringham, that God and Nature are synonymous, that dichotomies are artificial, and that only by living in accordance with nature—that is, with reality—can one find the fulfillment that one seeks. Perhaps this is the secret of Annie Spragg's contentment in Brinoë; certainly all of Bromfield's people who deny or distort natural tendencies and impulses are inevitably frustrated, emasculated, or destroyed. This concept, which is actually a low-level transcendentalism translated into a course of action, places Bromfield firmly in the main stream of American philosophical romanticism. At the same time it articulates a premise he had been fumbling for instinctively in his earlier novels, and it points out the future direction of his life and of much of his work. Increasingly both he and his characters seek that closeness with nature that provides, as he sees it, the only possible fulfillment in life.

In his previous novels he had intuitively felt this relationship, portraying it in his contrasts between believing and accepting, between the primitive and the sophisticated, and between the strong and the weak. In *Twenty-Four Hours* by these same contrasts, he shows for the first time that the difference lies in the ability or lack of ability to perceive, either instinctively or rationally, this ultimate truth. Bromfield's strongest people, on whatever level they find themselves, are those that follow nature. Not only do they accept natural values, but they believe in them strongly enough to follow wherever they lead. Persons on the middle social levels, because they have natural ability as well as aspirations, are those most likely both to perceive the difference and to have the strength enough to follow it. Those on the lowest levels, on the other hand, are usually lacking either in belief or in natural strength or intelligence, while those on the highest levels are normally so bound by appearance that they cannot perceive the truth of their very human natures, and by denying them they prevent their own ultimate fulfillment. At the heart of Bromfield's emerging philosophy is a strong faith in the American middle class. Thus the triumph of Melbourn is the corollary of the tragedies of the Towners and Rosa Dugan, and the city is the "armed barbaric camp" in which both groups struggle in "savage warfare continued day and night" to determine their destinies.

But the weaknesses of the novel remain to detract from its effectiveness both as a work of literary merit and as a vehicle for the expression of Bromfield's philosophical premises. The most serious of these shortcomings is structural. In adopting both the time limitation as a framework and the technique of closely related stories, Bromfield has forced himself to take refuge in contrivance and in sequences that not only do not carry conviction but are also unresolved. Thus the reconciliation of the Towners and the marriage of Dantry and Janie Fagan have all the ingredients of tragedy which Bromfield fails to explore; the romantic return of Hector's sister Nancy simply fails to come off; and the gangster, nightclub, and waterfront scenes are so unconvincing that they betray an almost complete lack of familiarity with their subjects. Finally, the happy endings that Bromfield provides for his naturally aristocratic heroes are products of arbitrary philosophic demands rather than reality, and the failure to explore the potential tragedies of Towner and Dantry imply happy endings that not only weaken his philosophic premise but lead to ultimate misinterpretation.

At the same time, in spite of its weaknesses, the novel has many merits. Characterization remains a strong point, and it does provide, as Henry Seidel Canby has commented, an admirable example of technical execution. As a panel novel more contained than the earlier sequence, it provides, too, as Canby further commented, a remarkable source for the social historian.[5] Finally, in providing a medium whereby Bromfield begins to articulate his statement of belief, it is a marked advance over his earlier works; and one suspects that this factor rather than its weaknesses in literary execution is the source of such adverse criticisms as those of Eugene Löhrke in *The Nation*. The holes exist not because he has cut "his cloth to fit the more glittering magazines and possibly Hollywood";[6] they are cut to fit his philosophy, and the great amount of disfavor the novel has met is not because of its alleged commercialism; it is because Bromfield's conclusions are based on what is ultimately tenuous evidence at best. But philosophic disagreement and literary artistry should not be confused.

The novel contains a number of interesting sidelights, some of which should provide fascinating material for the Freudian. Foremost among them are the anti-mother feelings that approximate hate in the portrayals of Hector Champion and Janie Fagan, both of whom see in their mothers the origins of their failures. More interesting for the literary scholar are the traces of the original panel relationship in the Ohio town background and in Jean de Cyon, who appears and disappears for no reason in the novel. And as a matter for speculation there is Bromfield's thinly disguised self-criticism of *Early Autumn*, referred to as *Burnished Autumn* and as written by a "precious young man" gifted with a style, "but somehow there was nothing behind the style."[7] It is interesting to note that the criticism is voiced by Hector Champion, who is not only one of the weak but is completely unable to distinguish between appearance—which in literature is style and form—and ultimate reality.

IV A Modern Hero

Bromfield followed *Twenty-Four Hours* with *A Modern Hero* in 1932, a novel in which he returned to the sweeping form that helped make his earlier novels successful. In this novel he attempted a full documentation of a man who has all the characteristics of the natural aristocrat except the vital one that insures success and fulfillment. The result, as Bromfield sees it, is inevitable tragedy; and his title is ironic just as the final tragedy is ironic because his "modern hero," in following the classic pattern of the American rags-to-riches myth, has success within his grasp when his basic confusion of values causes his destruction.

The story is that of a handsome, personable, and illegitimate son of a circus perfomer, Pierre Radier, who, by following closely the Horatio Alger formula for success, rises from a career as a circus rider to that of an industrial and financial magnate. Like Alger's heroes, Pierre is bound to rise because he has all the requisite talents and he uses them in ways that insure steady progress toward his goal of power and prestige. But Alger would undoubtedly dislike Pierre. As the novel opens, the circus has just played in Pentland, Ohio, where Pierre has met, loved, seduced, and abandoned Joanna Ryan, the daughter of a woman who is from one of the old families and a father who is an Irish drunk. Pierre debates marrying her, but recognizing its impossibility, he carries on with the circus life that he hates; Joanna, honest and respectable, marries a former suitor who loves her and is willing to accept her child.

In Chicago, Pierre sees his chance to escape the circus when the wealthy, aging ex-mistress of several rich men falls in love with him. He moves in with her, and she civilizes him while financing his career as partner to a talented mechanical tinkerer in a bicycle shop. His partner, Henry Müller, builds an automobile in which Pierre interests Homer Flint, a financial magnate from Pentland. Flint and Rader Motors is born after Pierre has Americanized his name to Paul Rader, left his mistress, and moved to Pentland. In order to consolidate his position, he marries Flint's daughter Hazel, a physically and emotionally weak girl who falls in love with him.

Joanna, meanwhile, had learned to love the farm, and she and her husband prospered while raising a large family of their own as well as Pierre's son. A chance encounter between Pierre and the boy begins a close relationship between them. The boy has Pierre's ruthlessness and charm without his intelligence, and he gets into a series of scrapes that Pierre shrugs off while Joanna and her husband look on helplessly. Finally, in a presumably secret financial venture, Pierre is ruined by his father-in-law, and the boy is killed in an automobile Pierre had given him. Taunted about the boy's death by his unbalanced wife, he strikes and kills her. In panic he runs to his old mistress in Chicago, where he is arrested by the detectives who had been waiting for him.

With one major exception the plot outline has all the ingredients of melodrama, from the classic seduction to the ultimate denouement. The exception is that Pierre is a likable villain, and his career is largely an amplification of the chance remark by David Melbourn in *Twenty-Four Hours* that such tactics are all right because everybody uses them. Pierre is a successful exploiter of women because they enjoy being exploited by him. His mistress aids him while she knows that by doing so she is losing him, and even Joanna makes room for him at the funeral after she knows that he has destroyed their son. Both of them are good women who are incapable of seeing that he lacks all human feeling—the shortcoming that prevents his fulfillment and insures his tragedy.

Pierre is Bromfield's view of the man who, with his father-in-law, Homer Flint, has despoiled the Midwestern countryside by introducing factories and fumes and who has made a mockery of its human and natural values as well. In spite of his foreign background Pierre is no less a despoiler than the native Yankee Congregationalist variety represented by Flint; but Bromfield has intensified this quality in Pierre both by the foreignness that he seeks to eradicate and by the fact that he is half Jewish, the bastard son of a European Jewish international banker. Again Bromfield has allowed the unnecessary and illogical Midwestern variety of anti-Semitism, with all its air of mystery and uncertainty, to creep in. It is significant, though, in this light, that while the good people such as Joanna never recognize his Jewishness, his fellow exploiters, the Americans Flint and Claire Benson, do so instinctively, although they do not object to it until what they see as its characteristics directly affect them. But the fact of Pierre's Jewishness as a motivating characteristic is a basic flaw both in the novel itself and in the entire structure of Bromfield's theory of exploitation versus achievement as a test for determining the nature of the natural aristocrat.

Indeed, the only distinction between Pierre's tactics in his rise to power and those of David Melbourn, as he recounts them in

Twenty-Four Hours, is the complete lack of human feeling that results from Pierre's Jewishness and leads to his downfall. Melbourn's rise is built on a situation no less shoddy than Pierre's exploitation of his mistress, and his treatment of Fanny Towner is as ruthless as anything Pierre has done; yet he is allowed to find fulfillment because he recognizes the value of love while Pierre is unable to. In this case Bromfield has again shown an inability or unwillingness to think his material through and to draw logical conclusions. As a result the novel becomes less a demand for "the reinstatement of discarded ethical commands," [8] as one of its reviewers saw it, than a poorly reasoned tract that bogs down in illogicality. Instead of defining the character flaw that leads to tragedy in the classic sense, as well as in the structure of his basic philosophy, Bromfield takes refuge in a folk legend that cannot be supported by his evidence.

The novel is further weakened by his characterization of Joanna as a woman who can wade through muck without being contaminated. Although we are told that she is strong and that she finds fulfillment in spite of the tragedies of her son's death and her husband's accident, Bromfield shows no such evidence in the novel. And her inability to see Pierre for what he is and to resist what she knows is corrupting her son makes her, in spite of the sympathy with which she is treated, a criminal fool without the talent either for good or for evil that marked her predecessors among Bromfield's women. Although drawn in the image of Hattie Tolliver, she emerges weaker than Fanny Towner.

In the background of the novel Bromfield has used much of the same material that he had in his earlier successes and as lavishly as he had before, but the basic weakness in characterization, the chief strength of the earlier novels, destroys the effectiveness that it might have had. As a result it is a character study that does not explore character; it is a study of exploitation that does not examine the problem; it is a study of virtue that confuses innocence with ignorance. The result is an artistic and philosophic failure that Bromfield should have foreseen.

To explain this failure after a period of solid if not great accomplishment and just before Bromfield's best work in *The Farm* is difficult at best, but its origins are evident as early as *The Strange Case of Miss Annie Spragg* when he began to attempt to formulate and articulate a philosophy of his own in his work. Perhaps he was attempting to rectify what several reviewers of the first four novels had commented was their chief shortcoming: lack of intellectual substance. The self-criticism inserted in *Twenty-Four Hours* tends to support this hypothesis; and, in the novels following his panels, he had begun to insert a more definite point of view. But in doing so in this novel, he had also come close to destroying his major strengths as a novelist.

Although much of the persistent critical disfavor toward Bromfield's work dates from this novel, the adverse criticism that it met was directed not at what Bromfield attempted and failed to do but at his philosophical premises. This approach has persisted until it has become a stereotype, although it is firmly rooted in the economic and social crises of the early 1930's. Led by the reviewers for *The Nation,* this criticism was essentially a demand that Bromfield focus upon "a rotting social system" rather than "a defect of personality," that he attack the "blindness that is a part and parcel of the whole competitive post-Civil War industrial system." [9] In effect it is a demand that Bromfield return to and expand on the satire and social consciousness that appeared in the background of the earlier novels; and because he did not join the ranks of the proletarian novelists of the 1930's he was regarded as a traitor who had sold out to commercialism. But Bromfield's talents did not lie in the direction of social criticism; they were in storytelling, in constructing of character, and in depicting of setting.

The defects in *A Modern Hero* arise from the fact that Bromfield used his talents so badly in what he attempted rather than in the failure to do what he had neither the talent nor the inclination to do. The faults in this novel lie in haste and in failing to probe as deeply into human character and the relationship of cause and effect as the material demands. There is evidence in works such as this to support the contention that he had become influenced by commercial considerations at the time, as had F. Scott Fitzgerald and so many others; and it is equally evident that he had no intention of demanding a social or economic revolution. But neither fact is fatal to any novel or to a novelist's career—as the mounting adverse criticism stated so bluntly. It is unfortunate, however, that the stereotype has endured, carried on by militant critics who ignore the many merits of the work he did both before and after he had allegedly become tainted with commercialism.

V *Rejection of His Time*

The philosophy of individualism tempered with a deep consideration for human values that Bromfield had begun to inject consciously into his work was at this time becoming an increasingly important concern in his personal life as well. Six years earlier he had rejected life in the United States because he felt that American life—dominated by the puritanism that manifested itself in prohibition, fundamentalism, and self-righteousness and by the materialism that had run rampant in its mad pursuit of things at the expense of human values—precluded any possibility of fulfillment. For a while, caught up in the social and intellectual ferment that he found in France and with his garden and his writing to turn to in refuge, he thought he had found fulfillment; but it became increasingly evident to him that he had not. The same madness that had brought Europe to the verge of total destruction only a few years before and that made a mockery of the virtues of courage and sacrifice demanded by its culture was making itself heard again in Germany and Italy, while France and England exhibited a frightening indecision and lack of concern.

At the same time Bromfield was caught up in a life that was fascinating and glamorous to a farm boy from Mansfield. As a celebrity in his own right, he attracted and found much stimulation with others. With the money to join them, he became increasingly conscious of the fashionable things to do; and so, like the others, he followed the seasons—to Switzerland for the skiing and to Brittany for the summer. In the background, as a place of security, he had the *Presbytère* and the garden at Senlis. But it was not enough, and he became increasingly aware that there was something lacking in his life, that there was something dangerously wrong both with the world and with the way he was living. His dissatisfaction was not mere restlessness, as trips in search of change proved easily; so he determined to find out in the only ways that he knew.

Recognizing that behind the almost ceaseless and purposeless activity of his bright, bitter circle the age he lived in was both potentially and actually destructive of all the things he believed in, he began to look for purposeful action and sought the construction of a world in which his values would predominate. He found both in two worlds: in the American Midwest of the eighteenth and nineteenth centuries, in which he believed the democratic dream had come closest to realization before the triumph of materialism; and in the efforts of modern India both to secure independence and to bring order and plenty out of chaos and poverty. But the first way, he knew, was gone forever, finding its only existence in the memories and ideals of people like himself and his father, Charles Bromfield, who, with Louis' mother, had joined the family at Senlis. As the dedication of *A Modern Hero* shows, Bromfield had begun to see his father in a new light. No longer was he to be the kindly, improvident man who existed in the shadow of his wife's indomitable personality and of the energy and determination of his children. Instead Bromfield began to see him as a builder rather than as a destroyer like Pierre Radier; in his efforts to bring honesty and democracy into politics and to restore exploited and abandoned farms to fertility, he was a man "who has always known the things that count." [10] And as such he was alone both in the world and in Bromfield's circle.

But the world in which the values of his father were important had been destroyed by industrialism and materialism, and it could not be reconstructed. At the same time, for all of the defects, writing *A Modern Hero* had taught Bromfield two things. It had taught him that to believe in the natural aristocrat of the new age, as he had attempted to portray him in David Melbourn of *Twenty-Four Hours*, was wishful thinking and that only a Flint or a Radier could rise to the top. Modern industry could never again provide the background for his ideas or his writing. At the same time it showed him, as he tried to recreate his father's values in the character of Joanna, that agriculture still demanded the same virtues. But that world was gone, and he believed that he could recreate it only in his fiction. So Bromfield began to write *The Farm* as its memorial, not yet aware that he might attempt to recreate that world in fact.

At the same time he began to look for constructive attempts to build a new world around him. He had talked without conviction of buying a farm in the United States, but he had dropped the idea as he became interested in the work in India and later in the cause of the Spanish Loyalists. Bromfield had become acquainted with a good many Indians, both in his travels about Europe and at Senlis; and he was impressed with the dedication and determination with which all of them, from students to officials, approached the problems of their country. Before he finished *The Farm,* a portrayal of the world as it had been, he determined to visit India and to see for himself the world of the future. In the winter of 1932 he, together with his wife and the ubiquitous George Hawkins, made the first of two trips. Between them he returned to America for the winter of 1933-34, during which time he toyed again with the idea of buying a farm. This period of searching, essentially a search for meaning and for roots, was to determine both the nature of some of his best fiction and the course of his life.

CHAPTER 4

The Meaningful Past

I The Farm

THE BEST of Bromfield's books and the most likely to endure is *The Farm*. In it Bromfield set aside the polemics that had proved detrimental to his work and to his literary reputation, and he allowed his natural talents and his own deeply felt sense of permanence and value in life to take command. At the same time he used the material and the people that he knew and understood best—the history and nature of his own family, in many cases almost literally transcribed—as the basis of the book, which resulted in an approach that both enhances and detracts from its effectiveness but without which it would be false.

The result is a book that is neither fact nor fiction, neither novel nor autobiography, but a form that draws from the materials of both. Like much of Sherwood Anderson's autobiographical work of the 1920's, it is a search for personal identification in the midst of a world gone mad and of a life suddenly become meaningless. It is in a sense an attempt to define and describe the transition in Ohio from wilderness paradise through a brief period in which Jeffersonian democracy came close to success only to succumb to the domination of commerce and industry. It describes too the decline of the human values that Jefferson and his followers advocated and tried to implant and bring to full growth in the territory beyond the mountains. In this sense *The Farm* is a social history.

But Bromfield's approach to this background of social change and his technique in constructing the book make it much more. As a basis he uses the history both of his own family from the time his great-grandfathers came across the Alleghenies to the Ohio country, and of the land itself as it changed from wilderness to a flourishing agricultural community and finally to an industrial city. In doing this, he uses human characters, of which there is a wide variety, all of them influencing the social, economic, and political changes that make up the transition; and he uses the farm and the town as characters as well as background before which the human characters play their roles. As a focal point for this panorama of change, Bromfield uses the perceptions of a boy who grows into manhood in the final years of the change. In effect, he reviews a hundred years of family and social history through the impressions, observations, and indoctrination that the boy receives from his earliest sense impressions to the last conflict that drives him from the land that had been the center of his family's existence for a century.

In the book Bromfield has said that he used factual material as far as possible, including family documents as well as the actual members and relationships of the family itself. Incidents and background, too, have been faithfully transcribed. Much of the earlier material, except for persons and outstanding or documented incidents, however, has been imaginatively recreated. Names, of course, have been fictionalized, but the characters themselves are real.

Although the plot is loosely chronological, it is not entirely so; for Bromfield moves freely from past to present in developing incidents and relationships. Yet it does move forward as changes unfold in the boy, the family, the town, and the countryside until the denouement. Then the new age with its new standards registers its irrevocable triumph, and the boy goes off to seek a new meaning and a new direction for his life; but he takes with him much that the new age had no use for.

The story opens with the appearance in Ohio of a man who carries with him the Jeffersonian dream of an agricultural commonwealth in which man can live in dignity and peace. Colonel MacDougal, a Marylander, is drawn as a man of The Enlightenment. Urbane, cultured, dedicated to the principles of Jeffersonian democracy and deistically inclined in religion, he arrives at the blockhouse in the wilderness convinced that here, if anywhere, the dream will flourish into reality. But before his land can be cleared, the forerunner of what is to defeat his dream arrives in the guise of a Yankee peddler. The Colonel turns aside, confident that such men, hypnotized by profits, will find no place in the new country; they are exploiters rather than the builders the land demands. But his friend, a Jesuit missionary and also an aristocratic intellectual, recognizes that the land has already been lost to the exploiters, as he leaves for the wilder, more remote desert land of Mexico.

The Colonel, already disillusioned with the majority of the settlers because they are simple, stupid, and dominated by the middle-class Protestant ethic, goes on nevertheless to found both a family and a self-sufficient rural manor. By 1850 he has seen his dream largely materialized in spite of the economic royalists whose machinations he had fled the East to escape. Turning over the affairs of the farm to his son-in-law, Jamie Ferguson, a young Scotsman from Pennsylvania who is possessed of a reverence bordering on mania for the land, the Colonel retreats to his books and to his philosophic speculations; he is confident in the security of what he has wrought.

But his son-in-law, young Johnny Willingdon's grandfather, is destined to see not only the dream disappear but the family driven off the farm by the effects of the changes of the post-Civil War years. The peddler whom the Colonel had encountered in the blockhouse also founded a dynasty that had entrenched itself in the town as strongly as the Colonel had entrenched himself in the countryside; and the times as well as the forces of economics and politics become dominated by the philosophy of the peddler. As Johnny becomes aware of the world around him, he finds that the farm—although it is still strong, serving as the secure family focal point that the Colonel had intended— is already threatened by the new age. For money—not strength, intelligence, and a sense of human worth—is the criterion by which its continued existence will be determined.

At the same time the battle between the two philosophies, essentially those of Jefferson and Hamilton as the family sees it, has been launched. Bromfield describes the effects of that battle on what had so recently been a wilderness. Perhaps the most effective contrast in the book is provided by three graphic descriptions of the area around Toby's Run, a stream that meanders through lowlands and swamps on its way to the river. As the Colonel sees it, it is clear, quiet and shallow, flowing between tree-covered hills, although it had recently acquired its name from an Indian chief who had gotten drunk at the blockhouse and drowned in it. Already, although the Colonel does not realize it, corruption has been introduced into the wilderness; the natural man, nature's nobleman, a concept which the Colonel found himself skeptically questioning, has also been corrupted by reality.

The second portrait of the stream, seen by Jamie, is of the area on the eve of the Civil War. The wilderness has disappeared, and on the hills surrounding Toby's Run the town has grown. But it is an orderly scene—not completely pastoral as the Colonel had dreamed but still dominated by the agricultural setting. The stream itself still flows free and clear through the swamps, although it has recently been bridged by a railroad that comes down the valley. The swamps were dominated by a strange castle-like house that rises in their midst from a hill, and in the town the sons of the peddler have introduced a store, a bank, and a factory.

The third portrait is of the area at the beginning of World War I. The stream has become an open sewer, carrying oil and debris from the factories and workmen's hovels that cover the filled-in swamps. Only by its name would either the Colonel or , Jamie be able to recognize it, but it is the scene that young Johnny has grown up seeing. The hills are covered by a city, and the city is dominated not only by its prosperous department stores and banks, but by a low row of ostentatious houses that stretch off to the west, away from the smoke and noise of the Flats that support them.

The nature of this change is the result of the battle that was predestined that night in the blockhouse. The Colonel and the peddler, the Jeffersonian and the Hamiltonian, the farmer and the shopkeeper, and the builder and the exploiter are many facets of the same dichotomy that Bromfield sees at the heart of the struggle to determine the nature of America in its maturity. The outcome, as the Jesuit foresaw in the blockhouse and as Johnny acknowledged as he left the farm forever, had been predetermined by the nature of the values held by each side and by the nature of the men themselves. The natural aristocrats, with their interest in man himself in his noblest sense, are handicapped because they cannot meet the exploiters on the field their opponents have chosen. They cannot use the weapons that are most effective, not because they don't understand them—although some, like Johnny's father are unable to—but because their very natures, their values, and their honor prohibit such ignoble means.

But the struggle between the two factions is only one facet of the book; it also provides the background for the intensely felt story of human relations that centers about Johnny's family, the Willingdons. Johnny's mother is the granddaughter of the Colonel; his father is the great-grandson of Jorge Van Essen, who had come over the mountains from Pennsylvania at the same time the Colonel had. Johnny's mother's line includes her father, Jamie Ferguson, a paragon of Scotch virtue. The maternal line incorporates stability, love of the soil, scepticism toward the delineations of theological structure, and intellectual inclination— all of which tend to set the family apart from the shopkeepers and from the masses of people of all backgrounds that have found their ways to the town.

In Johnny's father's line the German warmth and frontier Methodism of Johnny's great-grandmother, at war with the Calvinistic sternness and determination of his great-grandfather, a God-ridden New England schoolteacher, have produced a series of family tragedies. These culminate in that of the "Old Man," Johnny's grandfather, Thomas Willingdon, who, after a lifetime of bitterness and wandering, comes home to the son he has rarely seen, to die.

In the background of four generations of human fertility in a rich country are relatives so numerous that a reunion of his father's line incorporated more than a thousand persons. In the foreground is not the fertile mass that had peopled the Ohio country but the closeness of a group of individuals, many of them eccentric and priding themselves on their differences, but all held together by ties of traditions that are stronger than blood. As Johnny grows up, he finds he is tied as securely by these traditional bonds as he is by the two strains of blood that war within him: one demands something ever new; the other, that he give himself to the land.

The closeness of both blood and traditional ties is illustrated by the annual celebrations of the two great family holidays, Christmas and New Year's, at the two centers of family activity. Christmas is celebrated at the farm, the center of stability, plenty, and intimacy with nature. The tradition calls for an outpouring of the earth's abundance; that is, for all practical purposes, a pagan-like feast of thanksgiving for fertility and love. It is a celebration that ties the family, dozens of them at one table, to the past; because here, once a year at least, the Colonel's dream comes close to reality as his presence is almost felt in the huge room filled with the books, the furniture, and the blood that he had carried with him over the mountains.

The New Year's celebration is held at Trefusis Castle, the home of old Great-aunt Jane, in the heart of the Flats. Here, too, the gathering is tied to the past by blood and tradition; but, more importantly, it points to the future. The castle is an exotic place in which foreign artifacts and the fascination of great cities are as much part of the atmosphere as is the Colonel's presence on the farm. In the space of a week the dichotomy that Johnny feels in his own blood as well as in the world around him becomes personified in the two great family centers, just as they are in the people who dominate them: Great-aunt Jane at the Castle, and Grandfather Jamie at the farm. As Johnny remembers it, the two centers represent two facets of the same life—the good life of the past—as they join ranks despite their differences to fight against the new, in the form of factories, that encroaches on the castle in the Flats and that conspires against the farm in the demands of the market place.

The mystic sense in which the land and the past dominate the present is an outstanding characteristic of the book. From the lips of aged great-aunts, Johnny hears tales of factual people who have become legend in the Ohio country. Johnny Appleseed was not merely a mythological wanderer but the man who came to his great-grandfather's house, preached kindness, brought news, and planted the gnarled apple tree that stands over the Colonel's grave and the fennel that grows in dooryards. The Lost Dauphin, a romantic wanderer of the American frontier like Johnny Appleseed, was one of the prophets of the new country who peopled the stories of Aunt Esther. Together with tomahawking Indians and their degenerate, drunken, lost offspring, these characters fill Johnny's dreams as they tie his imagination closely to the countryside through which he wandered after them.

The past and the land are tied to the present, too, by the graves of the Colonel and his wife at the edge of the garden, and by the nearness—through the Colonel, Great-uncle Jacob and Jamie—of the eighteenth century to the present. The Colonel, a son of The Enlightenment, had lived to read Darwin and to see the federal government gain permanent dominance in the Civil War. Great-uncle Jacob, the Colonel's son, preserves the eighteenth century in his love of ease, his inaptitude for business, and his persistent curiosity that leads to inventions, both practical and not. Jamie, one of those who built the agricultural empire of the nineteenth century, had lived to see industrialism usurp its place and threaten to destroy it in the twentieth. The very soil that old Jamie lovingly tills is enriched by the Colonel's Jeffersonian dream as well as his body. And Jamie's dogged determination to refuse to give up is matched by that of the grandson at his side.

In the novel, too, is much commentary on the social structure of the new society as it is observed by a boy in the time of change and interpreted by an adult who recollects it. The nature of the changes is real to both because it has been dramatized by its impact on people they have known and on the land they have loved. The most vivid are the effects of change the boy had himself experienced. The nature of the changing attitude toward work is perhaps the most significant of these. Manual labor had turned a wilderness into civilization; and no matter what form work took, it was considered dignified. Jamie had been a farm laborer; Johnny did his share of the same work; the family had had a long line of farmhands and hired girls, all of them of native stock, who went through their tasks with dignity as well as efficiency. They were regarded as members of the family, and most of them went on to success of their own.

But suddenly, with the influx of the mills and the new people both from Europe and from the Southern hills, work lost its dignity and has become degrading. The old inhabitants feel that it is beneath them, fit only for the new; and the new, sensing that they are being degraded, go about their jobs in sullen inefficiency. The result is the introduction of class levels and antagonisms where none had existed before. Resulting, too, is an attitude that makes impossible an adaptation of the Jeffersonian ideal of an open society to the new age as it encourages a kind of shiftlessness that results from continued conviction of failure. Only in the few remaining tenant farmers like Hud Williams does the old tradition persist. A man of good stock, hard-working, and full of pride in his work's results, he is a strong contrast to both the degenerate and shiftless descendants of misfit Americans who resent the indignity of work, and to the newly arrived peasants who suspiciously and selfishly work for immediate material benefits rather than for the pride and dignity that have all but vanished from the countryside.

In the hierarchical structure made up of schools and churches there is also the evidence of the stratification and reinterpretation that have done much to destroy Thomas Jefferson's dream of equality of opportunity in a classless society from which its natural leaders emerge. Among the churches a social hierarchy that has nothing to do with theology has come into existence. Among the older denominations, the Congregational—the church of the oldest and best New England families—is most stylish; but it is closely followed by the Presbyterian, which is almost but not quite first rate. The cold decorum of these churches is followed on a much lower level by the Methodists and Baptists, the churches that were brought onto the frontier by the lower classes who became the Jacksonian Democrats. Like them, their churches were energetic and emotional, marked by the equalitarianism and primitivism that frightens the more respectable denominations.

Outside of this major hierarchical structure are the newcomer churches: the Lutheran, with its congregation of dull, honest, worthy, but not quite acceptable burghers; the Catholic church in the Flats for the Europeans; and on the square, rivaling the long-established Congregational structure, the very high-church Episcopal church of the new industrial and commercial aristocracy. The lines that separate the churches and their congregations are not theological, they are social; and the bigotry and intolerance that result from them is indicative to young Johnny of the basic dishonesty behind the protestations of jingoistic Americanism that is propagated from the pulpits and of the hypocrisy inherent in organized religion itself.

In the schoolyard, too, he finds the same perversion of democracy. The stylish fetish for private and boarding schools had not yet arrived in the town, and much is made of the democratic nature of the public schools that all attend. Yet he finds that there is the "good" school on the hill, which he and the other children of the old, good families and the new aristocracy attend; and there are other schools which descend in quality to the grimy building in the Flats. Even in the "good" Maple Avenue School, social stratification is apparent. The occasional poor child who finds his way there through an accident of districting is ostracized and tormented by pupils and teachers alike. It is in this school that Johnny finds out that, in spite of his membership in a good family, he is poor and hence kin to the others who have committed the crime of being failures. Only in retrospect, however, is the meaning of these observations apparent:

> Thirty years after he began to understand that what he witnessed was not simply a manifestation of childish cruelty . . . it was American. . . . It was the shadow of a philosophy which often enough took the place of religion. It was the principal motive of existence in a good many of those families who sent their children to the Maple Avenue school. One had to be successful, no matter how success was achieved. One must make money, no matter how one came by it. The only hell was poverty and lack of success, and the only heaven was material.[1]

Corruption, both of the Jeffersonian ideal and of the standards of simple human decency, has made itself felt on every level, and the result is a cruelty that is often more subtle but no less vicious than anything the world had known before. The peculiar nature of its viciousness lies in the hypocrisy that denies its existence while giving lip service to the traditional virtues.

Politics, prejudice, and economics come in for their share of attention; and each, in the experience of a growing boy in the formative years of industrial America, reveals a wide discrepancy between the American ideal and its practice. In politics the gap is perhaps widest; the Jeffersonian art of government by the many has become a manipulative and exploitative game for the few who control the machines and the purse strings. In his father's political experience the reality is made evident:

> James Willingdon left the bank for politics when two of the political bosses in the northern part of the State persuaded him that in politics there was a great future for him. Three things . . . led him to believe that he was the material they sought—his charm, his easy-going ways, and his wide acquaintance among the farmers. The Republicans already had such a man—handsome, simple, and willing to compromise. He came from the next county and already he had done much to help the "party," which meant that he voted as he was told by men who seldom held any office but stood in the wings, prompting and directing the performers. His name was Warren Gamaliel Harding. The

Democratic Party no longer held to its old-fashioned principles. In it too there were men who believed in tariffs and believed that "business" should be helped now and then discreetly and judiciously.[2]

In spite of the torchlight parades, the friendliness of campaigning in the country, the expounding of principles, and the heady stuff of victory, the reality makes itself felt. The father's honesty is seen as "eccentricity and pigheadedness"; his efforts to keep the morals of the market place out of government are futile; and his tenure in office is short: "he was not a politician in the meaning . . . of the New Era."[3]

In the areas of prejudice and economics something new had been added to the old. The chattel slavery that the Colonel and old Jamie had fought was gone, but it was replaced by an economic slavery that was "worse in the fundamental greed of its motives."[4] It was a slavery not restricted to Negroes but extended to all the unfortunate people in the Flats who were forced to work or who were unable to. Slightly higher in caste, but no less exploited when the opportunity arose, were the Catholics, the Jews, the Irish, and the Germans—all of them strange and alien in the town and hence to be tolerated only when they were useful. The mysterious difference of the Jews that manifested itself in warmth and sensuality in contrast to the coldness of the transplanted New Englanders was to set them forever apart, to give them their choice between exploiting and being exploited, and then to condemn them for emulating the tactics of the New Englanders.

The fear and greed behind this new kind of economic oppression were manifested in ways that varied from the extremes of the ridiculous reports about Popish plots for overthrowing the government to the harshly real symbols of the philosophy behind materialism. One of Johnny's most vivid memories is such a symbol; it is of the abandoned farms that line the country roads, their soil exploited and depleted and their houses falling down to be reabsorbed by the earth from which they came. Only Johnny's father is convinced that the exploited soil is worth saving.

The Farm is a strong book that provides one of the best accounts available, fictionalized or not, of the transformation of the Ohio country from a wilderness to a modern industrialized society. In spite of its rare historical errors—such as the reference to the existence of Fremont in 1814, when in fact that settlement was known as Lower Sandusky until 1842—it is important as a social as well as a personal document. As it documents the destruction of Jefferson's dream of a stable, agrarian, and democratic society in the new country across the Alleghenies, it also records the evolution of the pragmatic materialistic philosophy that dominates twentieth-century America. This is the concept that Bromfield, in common with the other disillusioned young romantics of the 1920's, rebelled against as he, like many of the others, went into self-imposed exile in the hope of escaping it. The book provides a view of the philosophy that Bromfield himself had rejected, and it also presents a nostalgic view of the intimate, man-centered world that he would prefer to see accepted in its place. He is convinced that that world once existed but that it is no longer possible to achieve in America.

In intent and in execution *The Farm* has much in common with Sherwood Anderson's *Tar: A Midwest Childhood;* but *The Farm* is much broader in scope. Both are attempts to recreate a way of life and a warm, intimate atmosphere that, in spite of its occasional brutality, is nevertheless both good and fulfilling. But whereas Anderson was interested in recreating a spiritual existence in which external atmosphere is important only because it is conducive to a life rich in feeling and in awareness of others, Bromfield in *The Farm* points out that the life of fulfillment can be found in a sensual partnership among the individual, his fellow men, and his natural environment. For Anderson the basic evil of the new age was that it isolated men from each other; for Bromfield it was that it dehumanized man as it forced him to abandon his closeness with nature. Both are romantic views that are part of the literary movements of rejection, rebellion, and liberation that marked the work of a generation disenchanted with the direction America had taken in the half century between the Civil War and World War I.

Although *The Farm* is a diffuse book that incorporates much of the social history of the nineteenth century, it is at the same time a well and tightly organized work that is deeply felt and personal. Its complexities are compounded by focusing on the growth of awareness in the boy as he moves from an initial sense of warmth and security in a friendly environment to the recognition of the warring strains not only within his family and himself but also in the world around him. This growth culminates in the romantic search in a hostile world for a renewal of that once-felt fulfillment that perhaps never had existed in fact. Although Bromfield had put his material together as well as it could be done, the richness and diffuse nature of the book led to charges of tediousness from his now perennial critical enemies on *The Nation's* reviewing staff.[5] Nevertheless, the book itself provides adequate evidence that Bromfield had not succumbed to commercialism in his serious work but that he was continuing his search for a personal philosophy based on values that he was convinced had been lost but had not lost their validity.

The Farm is a major step toward the formulation and articulation of that philosophy. Its beginnings were evident in the panel novels in his preoccupation with the conflicting values of external appearance and of personal fulfillment. His attempt to demonstrate that the ultimate kinship between man and nature culminates in God is a continued but unsatisfactorily presented manifestation of the same thing—as is his continued and often ambiguously and carelessly defined portrait of the natural aristocrat. *The Farm* is Bromfield's attempt to do two things: to determine, as nearly as possible, the origins of a philosophy that he had imbibed rather than consciously formulated; and then to define, as nearly as possible, the relationship between that philosophy and American life as he had known it. In order to do these things, Bromfield could turn only to his own youth and to the history of his family as he knew it—not in the attempt to vindicate a philosophy that had come under fire by the increasingly disenchanted critics of the left, but in order to understand it himself so that in the future the fiasco of *A Modern Hero*, which reflects an indecisive, basically confused Louis Bromfield, would not be repeated. In *The Farm* Bromfield's new sense of direction and of purpose becomes evident.

II   Here Today and Gone Tomorrow

At the same time that Bromfield found the intellectual and emotional stability that he had sought in writing *The Farm*, he was seeking a means of putting the results of that stability into practice in his own life. Disenchanted with the meaningless, ritualistic routine among the expatriates and anxious to commit himself to a way of life that would support his beliefs, Bromfield made the first of his trips to India and debated buying a farm there or in any one of a number of locations in America.

But then, after his American visit in 1933-34, he fled back to Senlis, away from an America which, in spite of the New Deal that he espoused, had not yet returned to the Jeffersonian faith. During this American visit, however, he put together *Here Today and Gone Tomorrow*, a collection of four short novels that had previously been published in magazines. He found himself unable to do any sustained writing at the time, in spite of the material that he had gathered in India. Moreover, he had an eager publisher to satisfy and the ménage at Senlis that he had begun to transport around the world was an expensive one.

All four of the stories are determinedly modern in setting and tone, and there is nothing so detrimental to permanence or that becomes dated and naïve so quickly. In the early 1930's their topicality was fresh, but in the 1960's his bootleggers, gamblers, and aimless expatriates—portrayed as stereotyped sketches rather than as characters in depth—retain as much significance as an aging comic strip. The first of the stories, "No. 55," is set in a New York speakeasy that is complete with plush furnishings, exclusiveness, a peephole, and all the rest of the appropriate accoutrements. The triteness of setting and characters might better have been used as a source of humor, as in Elmer Davis' *Friends of Mr. Sweeney*. Skillfully handled, the characters and the setting might even have risen above triteness to provide the material for tragedy, as Bromfield implies is the case. But they produce a story of trivial sentimentality rather than of honest emotion. Beppo, the owner of the speakeasy, gains the material wealth that he craves; but his heart of slightly tarnished gold and the death of his dream girl fail either to make him live or to provide more than material for plot manipulation.

The background and characters of "No. 55" set the tone for the volume, which focuses on the emptiness and meaninglessness both of the sophisticated life of post-World War I and of the people who are caught up in it. The book emphasizes, too, the fragility of the social and economic complex with which the new sophisticates have surrounded themselves. "The Listener," the story of a minister's elderly daughter who suddenly finds herself wealthy, carries the theme forward into the realm of international finance. The aging heiress, whose only interest in life is eavesdropping on conversations in fashionable European hotels, overhears a conversation between an international financier and his secretary. Angry because the financier had taken over her room and his secretary had struck her, she cables the secret to the New York firm that manages her finances. The resulting crash destroys both the broker and her own fortune. Unable to face poverty again, she dies quietly.

This story is superior to "No. 55" both in structure and in characterization, but it remains weak, primarily because Bromfield depends on carefully managed irony and coincidence for the working of his plot. Most important, however, is the fact that, although Bromfield was attempting to contrast the innocence of the old-fashioned and intimate world of gentility that existed before World War I with that of the new exploiters of the 1920's, the stereotyped characterizations of the banker and his mistress-secretary and the contrived nature of the plot make the story ineffective. Although Bromfield had employed the same sort of contrast successfully in his novels, it is not the sort of approach that can be effectively used in a shorter form.

"Fourteen Years After" is an attempt to capture the mood and the essence of the meaningless, affluent years after the World War I and before the Depression had restricted the activities of those fashionable people whose lives are spent in feverish movement by fashionable means of transportation from one fashionable place to another. The action of the story takes place aboard a new liner among an intimate group of first-class passengers on the last night out of a record-breaking run from Europe to New York. Bromfield does effectively capture the feverish desperation with which they seek fulfillment in the effort to deny both the feverish nature of their age and the transience of life, as he contrasts the prewar and the postwar worlds. But this story, too, is unsatisfactory because he has attempted to reinforce his theme through the superficial treatment of several subplots centering around the relations among the passengers, including a mechanically contrived love plot. As in the previous story, the relationships that might have been suitable for a novel are insufficiently developed.

The last story, "Miss Mehaffy," is the best of the collection, and this is primarily because Bromfield is not taking his subject matter so seriously as in the earlier stories but is having a bit of fun. Miss Mehaffy, the daughter of a Western badman and the proprietress of a house of joy, runs a quiet Midwestern tea-room but craves the excitement her parents had known. On a trip to New York to visit her protégé, one of the small-town beauty queens who flock to the city, she outgambles a profes-sional gambler and hospitalizes a gangster by hitting him with a bottle. Then she returns the girl, Baby Peterson, to her dull but safe hometown boyfriend.

In this story Bromfield uses many of the same ironies, incon-gruities, and stereotypes that he had in the earlier stories, but the lightness of tone and the deliberate exaggeration that he employs to show that the new East is simply the old West with-out either muscles or insight make it delightful. Miss Mehaffy herself is, in effect, a caricature of Bromfield's strong women, just as Baby, the gamblers, and the others are all spoofing por-trayals of types that Bromfield had regarded with too much seriousness before. The result is a more effective indictment of a meaningless age than any of the other stories.

On the whole, however, the collection did nothing to aid his critical reputation; it is unfortunate that he followed the sub-stantial achievement in *The Farm* with this volume. Although the novellas were written for a mass circulation magazine, to dismiss them as merely commercial is unjust. They are attempts to go beyond the commercial formula stories and to dramatize the emptiness in his age. But, in using the short forms, Bromfield is forced to focus on the surface of his subject matter rather than on its significance in permanent human terms. The result-ing stories are both superficial and dated, while the effective-ness that they might have had, had Bromfield treated their common themes in depth, is lost. Each novella is a condensed novel, and the broad approach that he employed in his novels cannot be effectively condensed.

III *The Plays*

Although Bromfield's earlier attempt to dramatize *The Green Bay Tree* was unsuccessful, he again tried to realize his ambi-tion to be a playwright in late 1934 and early 1935. He was determined to take Broadway by storm, using both the material and the technique of his novels; but, like his short stories of the period, both of his plays that were produced in the spring of 1935 were unsuccessful, and largely for the same reasons. The broad, sweeping approach of the novels was not adaptable to another form.

The first play, *DeLuxe*, was the product of a collaboration with John Gearnon. In the spirit of "Fourteen Years After," it attempts to capture the atmosphere of aimless, purposeless activity which characterized the affluent years before the Depression. Unfortunately, like the story, it loses its mood in a morass of meaningless action and contrived situations. More importantly, however, the portrayal of post-World War I decadence and opulence was simply uninteresting and seemingly trivial in a nation just emerging from the depths of the Depression.

The other play, *Times Have Changed*, closed almost as quickly. An adaptation of the material he had used in *Early Autumn* to the situation of Edouard Bourdet's *Les Temps Difficiles*, it depicts the attempt of a decadent New England family to revive the failing family fortune. Like *Early Autumn*, the play castigates the observance of form without either substance or belief and the subservience of reality to appearance. But the play itself is awkward and unwieldy, lacking the carefully controlled movement forward that the medium of the theatre demands.

Both the nature of the material that Bromfield had used during the early 1930's and the almost constant movement from France, to India, to America and back again indicate a dissatisfaction with his literary and financial success and with the bright, successful people with whom he surrounded himself. In his pointless and unsuccessful change of literary forms, in his preoccupation with the sterility of the fashionable existence, and in his attempts to find a basis for belief in *The Farm*, Bromfield was not only voicing his dissatisfaction with a life that he was beginning to recognize had no substance and was contrary to everything that he believed in; he was beginning a search for his personal identity and for a fulfillment that had eluded him. His introspection in *The Farm* identified the values that he believed meaningful, but they were impossible to achieve in the world he saw about him, a world that he had attempted to define in both short fiction and in plays. In his next work, *The Man Who Had Everything*, he turned to examine the irony of the position he found himself in, that of a man who denies the present, only to find that he can neither return to a past that is gone nor escape the future or his own nature.

IV The Man Who Had Everything

A longer version of a magazine short story entitled "Three Faces in the Mirror," *The Man Who Had Everything* is the story of a man who had nothing except fame, fortune, success, an attractive family, and all the other outward appurtenances of the good life. Basically it is a long dramatic monologue in which Tom Ashford, a successful thirty-seven-year-old playwright, recounts his dissatisfaction with his lot, his romantic eagerness to recapture the lost love of his youth, and his ultimate resignation to his fate as he allows himself to be convinced that he is in love with a fading actress. A thin book in substance as well as in size, it records simply and without amplification the impossibility of Ashford's recapturing his dream or escaping either himself or the age in which he lives.

The Man Who Had Everything epitomizes Bromfield's recognition that the romantic search must end in frustration in the twentieth century. The story of Tom Ashford, it is Bromfield's account of a man who had once, in the midst of war, known briefly peace, security, and love in a small villa between Paris and the lines. But the war and later his demobilization, together with his own drive to succeed, made it impossible for him to return, for it would be inconvenient and he wasn't entirely sure that he wanted to. But success came easily; and only after realizing the meaninglessness of his career, his sterile marriage, and the rather sordid affair he is engaged in, does he attempt to return to that peace and security: first, in spirit by purchasing the now-abandoned villa; and, second, by finding the girl whom he had loved. But the villa, with the conveniences and the bar that he adds, becomes a mockery; and the girl, a middle-aged bourgeoise widow, persuades him that he is in love with the actress who was his mistress. Spiritlessly agreeing, he returns to both her and his life.

The situation that Tom Ashford finds himself in is essentially the position that Bromfield feels to be his own dilemma. It is significant that Ashford does not question the value of his work or of his success. His real doubts and uncertainties stem from the life that his success has led to; as he walks the streets of New York alone, he reflects:

It was odd how as you won success you were removed little by little, imperceptibly, away from the rest of the world, until at last you lost the feel and even the savor of ordinary pleasant things and became a little inhuman, so that, even though you made a great effort to establish, once more a contact with the simple ones—the plodders, the dull ones, the failures—it was not possible. It was as if they would no longer accept you. Somehow you found yourself shut into a dubious fantastic paradise surrounded only by those who had succeeded.[6]

Ashford's rebellion grows out of the clash between solid, enduring human values that are firmly rooted in the earth and those that result from cleverness, material success, and a dedication to the appearance that is so often mistaken for reality. But this is the first time that Bromfield has portrayed the clash in terms of the life he rediscovered in writing *The Farm* and of the life he was leading at Senlis and elsewhere among the clever, fashionable, successful people who surrounded him. In *The Farm* he saw the clash as represented by that between the Jeffersonian ideals of the countryside and the Hamiltonian philosophy of the town; in *The Man Who Had Everything* he sees a similar clash in the difference between the physical appearance of youth in women like the actress who became his mistress, who defy and attempt to defeat nature, and in the maturity of the woman he had loved as a youth, who accepts age and the wisdom that comes with it. He sees it too in the difference between cleverness and intelligence and in that between a superficial relationship between man and nature through mere ownership of land and the reality that can be found only by working the soil in harmony with the natural order.

These dichotomies are at the heart of Ashford's dilemma, but his perception of them goes no farther than a vague sense that something is wrong and that somewhere in his idealization of the past he can find both eternal truth and personal fulfillment. But because his search is for a physical solution that has no existence and perhaps has never existed, it is evident that he has already been defeated. His decision to find meaning and love in his return to an empty life with a superficial actress is a hollow mockery of the permanence, the sense of identity, and the fulfillment that his wartime love had found in her life on the farm.

The ambiguous nature of the conclusion is evidence that Bromfield has not yet perceived the real significance of the problem that he presents. As he sees the problem in the novel, the past is gone; the world belongs to the clever people who attempt to mold life to their own ends rather than to the builders, those who mated their lives with the natural order. At the end Ashford convinces himself that somehow he can find natural fulfillment in a superficial existence. But even as he sends the cable that announces he is coming home, as he imagines a similarity between his shallow friend of the theatre and the perceptive middle-aged woman he once loved, he still lacks the belief that dedication demands.

The novel focuses on the problem that results in the tragedy of modern man, but Bromfield is at this point either unable or unwilling to admit that the tragedy exists. Instead, he allows his protagonist and a great portion of his reading audience to accept an apparent solution that can have no result other than that of hastening Ashford's inevitable destruction. In refusing to acknowledge the inevitable, or to allow his protagonist a bit more insight than the sheep that follows the Judas goat, he has simply compounded the confusion that surrounds appearance and reality. He has provided an apparently conventionally happy ending that, it is evident, is the result of wishful thinking—of belief in the world as it should be—rather than of either intellectual or emotional conviction. The resulting atmosphere of doubt not only detracts from the effectiveness of the novel and negates the irony of the title, but it is further indication of Bromfield's own uncertainty at the time.

Because the novel is essentially a monologue of a man who has been confused by appearance, Bromfield's usually clearly defined characters are hazy and distorted; they are seen only as two-dimensional projections on the screen of Ashford's consciousness. As a result, the intensity of Ashford's personal dilemma is heightened, not because he is beginning to perceive the reality behind appearance but because he is seeing what he wants to see. The resulting distortions of appearance are not glimpses of reality showing through; they are caricatures of appearance itself. Thus, for example, at the beginning he sees his friend Jimmie Beaumont, the producer of his plays, as a manifestation of the superficiality inherent in the life he despises; at the end, he sees Beaumont as the solid core of intrinsic worth in the life he is returning to. In spite of Beaumont's existence in Ashford's mind, he does not exist as a person; his function is as a focal point for whatever Ashford convinces himself to be true.

Despite the effectiveness of the internal monologue technique, *The Man Who Had Everything* is far from Bromfield's best work, although it has more substance than his short stories or the novellas in *Here Today and Gone Tomorrow*. It loses effectiveness because of the unreal conclusion, and the structure of the story itself suffers from the tricks that the technique depends upon for such mechanical aspects of the plot as the passage of time. The resulting impression is that the novel is contrived in spite of the intensity of Ashford's emotion and the thoroughness with which his perceptions filter the world. Bromfield's first major departure from his own role as omniscient author to active participant is, from the point of view of literary art, unsuccessful in spite of his efforts to define a man's indecision and search as he experiences them himself. Had Bromfield moved as freely as he normally does in his novels, showing the depth of Ashford and of his other characters, it might have been successful.

The book is, however, a clear portrayal of the sense of purposelessness and meaninglessness that dominated Bromfield during this period. His rejection of the easy money in Hollywood, his restless movements over three-quarters of the world, and his off-again on-again decision to buy a farm and return to the life he had left behind almost twenty years before were motivated by the same sort of search for values that motivated Ashford. The ambiguous uncertainty with which Bromfield attempted to find an answer is clearly portrayed in Ashford's view of Jimmie Beaumont, a graphic picture of Bromfield's manager-friend, George Hawkins. The uncertainty and ambiguity with which Bromfield continued to regard Hawkins, as a sympathetic friend on the one hand and then as a ruthless exploiter, is touchingly described by Ellen Bromfield Geld.

But out of Bromfield's trips to India he began to see a way out of the seemingly unsolvable dilemma of meaninglessness. In both Europe and America he felt that materialism, the goal as well as the source of the exploitation that had destroyed the old values, had already made inevitable the destruction of the Western world. But in India, among the few who had cast aside the old entanglements of superstition and at the same time had refused to become enamored either of things or of power, he found people who accepted and believed in the values that he had thought were destroyed forever. Like Jefferson and the Colonel, this minority was fighting to bring an ideal into reality; and in spite of the puritans, the priests, and the exploiters who fought desperately, they promised to be successful. At first Bromfield was determined to join them; he decided to buy a farm on the Malabar Coast and to settle there permanently. But instead, in the effort to define the thing that these people were attempting, he started a new novel. It took over four years to complete; but, when it was finished, Bromfield finally saw an answer to his dilemma.

The Meaningful Present

IN INDIA of the 1930's, a sub-continent that was neither a nation nor a country but a vast mass of human beings struggling with and against each other in the effort to forge a common identity and a common purpose, Bromfield found epitomized the human dilemma of the twentieth century as he saw it to be. In India, a land torn between superstition and enlightenment, between an inhuman past and a humane future, between the material pragmatism of the West and the mystic resignation of the East, he saw the same battle waged with the promise of success that he had seen lost in America in the years between the Civil War and World War I.

I The Rains Came

In *The Rains Came* Bromfield attempts to describe the course of that battle as it is waged between groups of men who, through conviction, apathy, or fear, have espoused varying aspects of the many struggles that make up the birth pangs of modern India. He focuses too on the same conflicts as they take place within individuals themselves who strive to free a nation and to free themselves. The result is Bromfield's most consistently executed novel, and it is also his most fully developed statement of his belief in man's potential.

The background of the fictional state of Ranchipur provides an appropriate site for the struggle between the old and the new and for the definition of the nature of the conflict. Ranchipur is an enlightened state ruled by the benevolent and humane, wealthy and cultured Maharajah and Maharanee. Both are dedicated to eliminating the misery that stems from poverty, religious superstition and prejudice, and the ravages of disease. They are striving to secure freedom, security, and happiness for their people.

In the foreground of this determined, directed struggle for human dignity, Bromfield personalizes the forces that carry on the battle on the sides of both light and darkness, in an array of characters far larger than any he had attempted to use before. But neither struggle nor forces are expressed in entirely symbolic terms, although his people are clearly symbolic. The struggle, as Bromfield portrays it, is a human one, and his people are human beings; they are both the source of the struggle itself and the determining factors in its eventual outcome. In spite of the fact that he sees the struggle itself in epic proportions, the novel is an individualized story of the human entities that he sees as the source of human destiny.

In the foreground of the novel are two men in their midthirties, Tom Ransome, a Westerner of English-American descent, and Major Safti, a Brahmin physician and surgeon. In these two characters Bromfield demonstrates the nature of the struggle both as it has been lost in the West and as it is still waged in the East. He also points out that the individual may yet save himself, regardless of the outcome in society at large, by refusing to surrender to the demands of society and by carrying on the fight with determination and dedication. Fulfillment, he shows, lies not in the end of life or in what one achieves but in the integrity with which one lives.

Tom Ransome is Bromfield's most fully developed and most acceptable male character; as he is portrayed in the novel, he is an extension of Tom Ashford, the man who had everything—but after his inevitable realization that he still had nothing. Spiritually sick and at times almost dead, Ransome, the wealthy grandson of a Nevada silver millionaire and of English aristocrats, has taken refuge in Ranchipur. There he exists as a spectator who admires the attempts at social progress but makes no effort either to understand or to aid in the struggle. The war and its aftermath of materialism and excess have left him without faith or hope in himself or in the outcome of a struggle such as he had already seen fail in the West. As one of its casualties Ransome is one of the walking wounded who has neither the strength nor the faith to do more than exist.

Major Safti is a medical soldier who still has both strength and faith, based on modern science and in man himself. Having rejected the superstitions surrounding the caste structure and the sense of hopeless resignation that dominates so much of the East, he is determined to build a new society in which the individual, regardless of background, is supreme. He has faith in the ultimate success of his cause in spite of the accumulated obstacles of thousands of years of human history. In the course of the novel, both Ransome and Safti come to understand the nature not only of the struggle but of man himself. For Ransome, the man of the West who is tired and faithless, the immediate task is to regain, through his own efforts, both faith and the will to live after he has begun to perceive the meaning of integrity and dedication. For Safti the task is not only no easier, but actually more subtle and complex. Safti must consciously struggle against the persistent despair of the East as he finds it in himself in moments of personal crisis. But in both cases Bromfield demonstrates that with strength and faith the ultimate triumph is the individual's; multiplied, it is man's.

These struggles, which are largely internal, provide a strong contrast to those among the people surrounding both men as well as to the eternal struggle to subdue a nature that in India is relentless and overwhelming. Among the people caught up in the struggles, Bromfield sees three major types: the builders, who have faith both in themselves and in the worthiness of their goals; the exploiters, who, no less dedicated, are the sources of both physical and spiritual destruction; and the defeated ones, who have seen or have allowed the ultimate triumph of the exploiters. Among these three types, divided almost equally between East and West, Bromfield has drawn a wide variety of characters, all of them individualized and at the same time indicative of the many forms which that building and that exploitation take. In these characterizations he indicates that these categories are not fixed; the individual, through the strength of his own will and his gain or loss in personal integrity, can pass freely from one category to another if he so chooses. But the price of such a change is high; often it is at the cost of one's life. But regardless of outcome, the builders find fulfillment in the way they live.

Although he pictures the West as defeated while the East is still carrying on the struggle, Bromfield points out in an effective series of character comparisons and contrasts that many people of the West are dedicated to building and that many of the

Easterners have already joined the ranks of the exploiters or have been defeated. In Ranchipur, under the sponsorship of the Maharajah and Maharanee, those westerners who want to work for the establishment of human dignity are provided with the opportunity, the means, and the necessary encouragement. Those who do not are merely tolerated if they are, like Ransome, demoralized refugees; they are condemned if they are exploiters.

In his introduction to the portion of *The Rains Came* that he selected for inclusion in Whit Burnett's *This Is My Best,* Bromfield stated that he had selected the excerpt because it best illustrates his fictional theory of the proper relationship between characters and setting:

> I seek . . . to deal with character and the interplay of characters against a background or environment which in itself plays a definite part in their motivation and the moulding of their thoughts and actions. For me characters must not be imposed upon a plot but rather the *story* must grow out of the characters, their environment and background.[1]

In the relationship between the immediate setting of Ranchipur in the foreground of a world in turmoil and the people who find themselves in Ranchipur—either by design or by accident—Bromfield illustrates the workability of that theory both in relationship to character and plot development and to his statement of theme. Among his people are two contrasting American missionary families: the Smileys, who are less interested in the theological nature of conversion than they are in leading the Indians to human dignity; and the Simons, who are more interested in their relationships with the exploiter class of the British and the Home Mission Board than they are with either the service of God or the needs of man. In the Smileys—man, wife, and indestructible old Aunt Phoebe—Bromfield returns to the same concept that had motivated Olivia Pentland in *Early Autumn:* a faith that transcends personal needs or ambitions and that finds its justification in dedication to those elements in life that are worthy of both preservation and extension. In their preoccupation with their people, the Smileys have drawn their inspiration and example not from either the mission board or the righteous pronouncements of church or Old Testament but from the simple injunctions of Christ to love.

The Simons—father, mother, and two daughters—are what

Bromfield conceives as "modern missionaries." As such, their motivation stems largely from what he feels is the sickness of the West: a lack of faith in either God or man and a concern with the externals of appearance that dominate both theological and social relations. The result for the Simons—and especially for Mrs. Simon, a relic of the American Southern myth of a society that never was—is an attempt to emulate the minor members of the British exploiting class and to exploit their position in Ranchipur for personal aggrandizement, even at the expense of their roles as missionaries. The Smileys are builders; the Simons are symptomatic of the sickness of the West.

In the character of Fern, the older daughter of the Simons, Bromfield demonstrates that the difference between membership in the builder class and in the exploiter class lies in human strength of character and integrity. Raised in an environment dedicated to external appearance and selfishness, Fern learns, through an attempt to exploit Ransome that turns into love, that personal fulfillment is not achieved through selfishness but through service. Her consequent rejection of her own family as she acquires the faith and integrity of the Smileys gives her life direction, purpose, and meaning. This concept recurs in the book, especially in the portrayal of Lady Esketh; for Bromfield points out that the stranglehold of environment may be released through a personal, essentially selfish love that can provide the basis for a universal love expressed in a dedicated will to fight.

Among the lesser characters of both East and West, Bromfield continues his delineation of the dichotomy that he sees as dividing men and as causing the basic struggle. Among the builders who for various reasons have taken refuge in Ranchipur, Bromfield emphasizes the women because they, rather than the men, have the single-minded devotion, the strength, the faith, and the integrity that are necessary to resist the seduction of materialism and the apathetic sickness that has emasculated men like Ransome. The Englishwomen Miss MacDaid, the nurse who has spent her life in the East, and the pathetic Miss Dirks, the schoolteacher; the American Aunt Phoebe; and the Indian Maharanee are additions to Bromfield's long gallery of strong, determined women.

Intolerant of those who lack her strength and determination, Miss MacDaid is motivated by her contempt of the weakness resulting from the religious and superstitious background of the

Indians and by the uncertainty of her emotions toward Major Safti. She dominates the hospital and the lives of the men with whom she is associated, and she determines to protect Safti from an emotional and sensual entanglement that she knows will destroy him. But, whether because of her own unrequited love or his value as a surgeon—a decision she refuses to make—she finds herself in a moment of weakness slipping into the very kind of superstition that she condemns. There is much of Emma Downes in Miss MacDaid, and there is much, too, of Ellen Tolliver.

Miss Dirks might have been another Miss MacDaid had she been able to escape completely the effects of the puritanism in her background that had come close to destroying both herself and the weak Miss Hodge, her dependent shadow. But in spite of the puritanism that she is afraid to defy because doing so would destroy her friend, she finds within herself the strength to rise above death and to go to it willingly in the pursuit of her duty.

Aunt Phoebe and the Maharanee are Bromfield's most complete portrayals of the strong woman. Aunt Phoebe is an American Midwesterner. The daughter of pioneers, she comes to India because in her small Iowa town there is nothing to challenge her strength or to stimulate her imagination. The Maharanee, one of the wealthiest women in the East, rejects a life of luxury on the Riviera in order to match her strength against those forces that threaten to destroy her people. In spite of the wide differences in background, the two women recognize their kinship. Aunt Phoebe, Bromfield remarks, is the last of the democrats and is in many ways a reincarnation of the Colonel who had established *The Farm;* the Maharanee, he asserts, is the last of those who accept the responsibility of leadership.

Bromfield's men characters exhibit the same combination of strengths and weaknesses that have characterized those in his earlier novels, but in *The Rains Came* there is an important difference. Here, for the first time, he makes it clear that they can—if they have the strength and the integrity—overcome defeat as well as the seductiveness of materialism and the enfeeblement of superstition. In Ransome and his Indian counterpart, Mr. Bannerjee, Bromfield points out that the ability to rise above crisis, or above the weakness that forces one to succumb, is the determining factor. Both Ransome and Bannerjee are urbane, educated, wealthy men of good families. Caught in the flood at

Bannerjee's home, Ransome finds himself unable to take command of himself because he is drunk; Bannerjee takes refuge in the superstitions of his religion. Both men are ashamed of their weaknesses, but Ransome's shame leads him to determined action that results in eventually overcoming it, while Bannerjee, unable to resist, is destroyed.

Among the lesser characters, Bromfield shows both builders and exploiters from West and East, reserving his most severe indictment for those who are too blinded by selfish interests based on appearance to find within themselves the integrity needed to build rather than to destroy. With the exception of Mr. Bannerjee, these people are exclusively western. Lord Esketh, who raised himself from an ironmongery to the peerage through dedication to the pursuit of money and power, regardless of means, finds in Ranchipur the meaninglessness of money in itself and the ultimate indignity of a degrading, lonely death: Bauer, the Maharajah's attendant, rejects human feeling in favor of a less ambitious but no less materialistic goal, only to meet a similar kind of end. Mrs. Simon seeks social prestige and gains ignominy; Mrs. Hoggett-Clapton, the wife of the bank manager, becomes a common drunk, a target for ridicule. In each case the lack of faith and integrity makes inevitable the loss of their goals and their inevitable destruction.

The most ironic portrayal in the novel is the similarity between Major General Agate, the Kiplingesque empire-builder who has devoted his life to preserving and extending the British Empire, and Lord Esketh, who has just as devotedly expanded its commercial power. In spite of their apparent success and their reputations as builders, Bromfield portrays both as men who have destroyed the empire: Agate, in his blindness to the realities of human relations that possess the meaning which mere political ties cannot; and Esketh, in his confusion of ruthless exploitation with solid, meaningful construction. Both men, blinded by appearance, are equally blind to the fact that the true builders see them as symbols of decay, degeneration, and death.

Bromfield reinforces the irony of this contradiction in the efforts of the defeated refugees from the West to seek fulfillment through carnality and in the destruction of the dam that provides electric power to Ranchipur. Ransome, Edwina Esketh, more properly Lady Esketh, and Maria Lishinskaia, a White Russian refugee, all jaded and tired, seek permanence in the body and in the sexual act, the only tangible proof of existence and meaning that they have left. But the body itself is impermanent and the pleasures of the sexual act are fleeting; the appearance has deluded them until, in moments of crisis, each of them is forced either to probe beneath the surface for meaning and fulfillment or to accept the fact that in sensual pleasure there is nothing. Both Ransome and Edwina meet the test, are purged, and find and accept the underlying reality that saves them, even though Edwina dies as a result. But Maria, unable to accept the meaninglessness of the physical in spite of the harsh evidence that Bauer presents her, is forced to destroy herself. Preoccupation with the physical—deemed good by the decadent West, just as material building is considered praiseworthy—is shown to be a hollow shell of appearance, which masks lack of faith and integrity.

The dam and its electric plant are the pride of Ranchipur, and as such they are considered mandatory sights for visiting dignitaries along with the schools and the hospital. All these things are tangible proof that progress is being made, and all of them are considered symbolic of the successful marriage between western technology and eastern vision and strength. But the technician who constructed the dam, a builder in the tradition of Lord Esketh and General Agate, had gone on to greater success as a manipulator and builder of financial empires; and the dam, an apparently solid and permanent structure, hides behind its formidable appearance the shoddy construction and dishonest materials that are at the heart of anything constructed by such people. The dam's collapse—causing the flood that is the crisis of the characters' lives as well as the climax of the novel—is also the symbol of the collapse of Oriental faith in western technical competence and achievement. As the flood causes the collapse of western mechanical civilization and of the older traditional Indian civilization, the only remaining symbols of man's enslavement to either way of life are the head of the cast-iron statue of Queen Victoria that stands above the flood to catch floating debris and the smoke of the roof-top funeral pyres of Indian superstition.

The world of the flood is entirely primitive, and those who are strong enough to insure their own survival and to make order out of chaos find fulfillment and freedom in usefulness—no matter how menial—and in dedication to building a new society that is free of western fear and hypocrisy as well as of eastern fear and superstition. At the same time those lacking the necessary strength and integrity, unable either to save themselves or to find fulfillment, are themselves destroyed, either physically or symbolically. As Ransome, Fern, and Edwina find the meaning they seek, as Safti and Miss MacDaid find justification in their own strength and skill, as the Maharanee and Aunt Phoebe find the renewal of youthful strength because their talents are needed, and as the Smileys find their faith in the dignity of man vindicated, Mr. Bannerjee falls prey to his fear, Mrs. Simon is left pathetically alone and helpless, and her friend Mrs. Hoggett-Egburry is unmasked as a fraud. In two of the revealing minor tragedies of the crisis, Captain Harry Loder, almost a caricature of the beefy insensitivity of the Indian Army officer, finds the dignity of death while phlegmatically if unskillfully performing his duty; and Miss Murgatroyd, the spiritually deformed Anglo-Indian spinster, succumbs to human prejudice and ignorance.

The most ironic result of the crisis is the death and cremation of Lord Esketh. A victim of the plague as the result of his visit to the Maharajah's stables in his failing effort to prove that money can buy everything, his death not only frees Edwina but frees his wealth that it may do good instead of evil. The necessary burning of his body for sanitary reasons, without either ceremony or regret, provides Bromfield with the opportunity to contrast effectively the meaningless rituals that would have followed his death had it taken place in the West.

In the background of the novel Bromfield finds opportunity to show, through the speculations and observations of his characters, further evidence to support the validity of his thesis. He comments that the nature of the "Indian question" is actually no different from the struggles of any other people for the right to direct their own destiny; it is the product of petty bureaucratic western minds that are unable to understand the demand for human dignity, an inability that has destroyed faith in the West. The "India sickness" is a product of the country itself, stemming from the degeneracy of a once-stimulating religion that has lost its potency and from a population that has become a mysterious, all-consuming mass. Both "question" and "sickness" combine to produce an atmosphere of fear much like that of the western Dark Ages.

At the core of the resulting problem, as well as of the many individual problems that are manifested in the novel, is the nature of man's relationship to his fellow men. Bromfield maintains that human relationships, from marriage to government, should be based upon humility and understanding rather than upon the pride, the passion, and the ruthlessness that often characterize them and lead to inevitable spiritual as well as physical destruction. The builders in the novel are those who recognize this distinction both instinctively and intellectually; as a result, they find the fulfillment they seek in their relationships with other men. Conversely, the exploiters do not; hence they bring about inevitable destruction.

India in the novel is merely a contemporary manifestation of the real battle that Bromfield sees as the nature of man's life as he had been describing it in his fiction from the beginning of his career. In *The Rains Came* he recognizes for the first time, however, that it is a universal problem rather than one peculiar to middle-class Americans in a mass, technological society, as the earlier novels assert. It is the age-old attempt to reconcile man's spiritual aspirations with the limitations of his body and his physical environment, in the course of which so many idealistic searches for meaning have been undertaken; in Bromfield's case, as in that of so many others, it results in an attempt to define means of penetrating physical appearance in order that one may approximate identification with an underlying spiritual reality.

Although Bromfield's emphasis upon the survival of those who have both the strength and integrity to reject physical appearance, together with the destruction of those who cannot, seems to imply a sort of idealistic natural selection, actually his emphasis upon moral fitness as the criterion for fulfillment is more nearly related in concept to the traditional theology that he rejects. It is a portrayal of the world as Bromfield would have it—a world in which his natural aristocracy would survive and triumph—rather than the world that he has described in his previous novels, especially in *The Farm*, in which the harsh reality of the material world produces spiritual alienation.

The Rains Came is the most fully developed fictional presentation of Bromfield's personal philosophy that he was ever to write, and not until the spate of nonfiction that he produced in books and articles during the 1940's and 1950's was this expression to be surpassed. All the old ingredients that he had dealt with in varying degrees in the earlier works are in this novel. Those of his people who find fulfillment are the natural aristocrats; indeed, Aunt Phoebe and the Maharanee are the most carefully delineated examples of the type that he was ever to produce. The belief that man must work in harmony with nature if he is to survive has become so particularized that Bromfield comments that the people are what they are because of the food they eat, thus pointing out the specific direction that much of his later work was to take. In the novel he makes this principle graphic. The higher-caste Hindus, bound by religious taboos that restrict their diets, are weak; the Untouchables and the enlightened members of the higher classes are physically strong and free of the "India sickness" of the mind.

Bromfield's most severe castigation is reserved for the manipulators, the exploiters whom he had condemned from the very beginning; but this, too, has taken on universal implications. No longer are they the despoilers of a pleasant Ohio valley or those who prevented the realization of the Jeffersonian dream. In *The Rains Came* they have laid waste half of the world, they have directed its technology toward destruction in one major war that has left the West a spiritual wasteland—all in the name of sacred profits—and they are threatening the other half of the world. The portraits of Lord Esketh and his minor cohorts are the most vicious Bromfield has ever done; even in the horror of Esketh's death there is no trace of human sympathy; instead there is an air of righteous retribution. This, too, is a point of view that Bromfield was to continue to hold, especially as World War II came closer to reality.

Finally, Bromfield uses the setting of Ranchipur to give a reality in time and place to his Jeffersonian dream of a stable, enlightened society in which human dignity reaches its apex of recognition and attainment. Intrinsic rather than superficial worth is recognized and rewarded; the cultural as well as the humane values are cultivated; and government, the proper province of the natural aristocracy, provides a loose paternal supervision. But all of this can come only after the revolution that purges society of its apathy and sickness. After men like Major Safti and his friend Colonel Moti, those dedicated equally to the ruthless destruction of germs and superstitions, and after the forces of nature have done their work, the new society can be brought into being.

A novel as broad and varied as *The Rains Came* almost inevitably has weaknesses, but they are neither so numerous nor so serious as in those novels in which Bromfield was approaching and formulating the statement that provides its basis. Characterization is strong, invariably so in the prominent western characters, much as in the pattern of the earlier works; but many of the lesser characters as well as most of the Indians are types rather than individuals. Only once, in fact, in Major Safti's struggle with himself, does Bromfield come close to understanding the Indian character. Although the Maharanee is a complete and acceptable portrayal, she is another representation of Bromfield's universal strong woman rather than a recognizable Indian.

Nevertheless *The Rains Came* is a major achievement in its delineation of the nature of the sickness that has dominated so much of the twentieth century and in its portrayal of modern India; it has, in fact, found more acceptance among modern Indians than E. M. Forster's *A Passage to India*. Because of excellent technical execution in structure and style, the book is, with the exception of *The Farm*, the best of Bromfield's novels, and in total impact it should rank high among the books of its time.

Although the book was well received in England and France as well as in India, it received a cool reception among the major American critics who for the most part attacked it because they found Bromfield's philosophy tinged with an apparent fascism that he neither presented nor implied. Hollywood's choice of this book as the basis for a much-publicized spectacular production raised the old charges of commercialism, although the resulting distortions of emphasis in the motion picture had very little to do with the nature of the novel. Its easy adaptability to another medium is testimony to Bromfield's powers as a storyteller, but it is unfortunate that it has resulted in permanent but unjustified damage to his literary reputation.

In the months following the publication of *The Rains Came* Bromfield found little time to devote to writing or to India as it groped its way toward national identity. The series of European crises that had begun with Adolph Hitler's accession to power in 1933 had accelerated; the Rhineland had already been re-militarized; Ethiopia had been conquered; the Fascist rebellion had broken out in Spain. Now Hitler had begun his threatening gestures toward Austria, culminating in *Anschluss* on

March 13, 1938; the war in Spain began to take on international proportions; and Czechoslovakia took its place on the Nazi agenda for conquest. Recognizing that the inevitable was at hand, Bromfield devoted his writing and organizing talents to what he saw as the immediate problems; at the same time, he made the decision that he had been pondering for years and that was to dominate the rest of his life. He had already attacked the philosophy of appeasement and peace at any price, as well as the belief that one could do business with Hitler, in an article for the London *Daily Herald*. Maintaining that Fascism rather than Bolshevism was the immediate danger, in it he denounced the British leaders for their refusal to recognize the nature of Hitler's philosophy.

In the summer of 1938, recognizing that the imminent outbreak of war would make Senlis, on the traditional military route between Paris and the German frontier, untenable, he made arrangements for his family to return to America; but he had no plans himself for a permanent return at the time. As president of the Emergency Committee for American Wounded in Spain he was busy raising funds for and arranging the return to America of the members of the Abraham Lincoln Brigade who had begun to figure prominently in the casualty lists from across the Pyrenees. For this work he was made a Chevalier of the Legion of Honor. At this time, too, he began an article, later published as a pamphlet called *England, A Dying Oligarchy*, in which he continued to attack the British government as he had in the article for the *Herald*.

II   *The Return to Ohio*

Meanwhile, in November, 1938, as the Spanish Civil War neared its conclusion in a triumph for Fascism, he returned to America to establish his family in Ohio. He planned to return to France to take up his work the following spring; but his French friends, especially the curator of the *Abbaye de Challis* at Senlis, advised him to stay in America where he could use his abilities to alert the American people to the imminence of war. Bromfield refused to accept the advice at the time; but, when he saw the rolling hill country of Richland County for the first time in years, he knew that he had come home to stay. There he felt the sense of permanence and continuity that had

eluded him for so long; and, on a cold winter day when he
rediscovered Pleasant Valley, he told himself, like Brigham
Young in Utah, that this was the place.

Having made his decision as abruptly as he had made the
decisions to leave Mansfield, to establish himself in France, and
to become a successful writer, he bought three adjoining farms
and was determined to complete the dream of restoring them to
fertility that had ended in frustration twenty-five years before.
Throwing himself into making plans, he named the farm "Malabar" after the coast that he had decided was second in beauty
only to the Ohio hill country. He began the restoration of land
that, like a French peasant, he could hand down to his children,
and he began to design the "Big House."

Meanwhile, however, he had not forgotten his promise to tell
the European story in America. Sending George Hawkins back
to France to close the *Presbytère* at Senlis and to ship his
accumulation of French antique furniture to America, he published *England, a Dying Oligarchy,* and he also began a series
of speeches about the European crisis that took him all around
the United States.

III   England, A Dying Oligarchy

England, A Dying Oligarchy is an attack on what Bromfield
saw as the tragic folly of the British government in its reluctance
to seek a showdown with Hitler, and it also attacks the shopkeeping exploitative philosophy of the Lord Eskeths, who had
laid waste to much of the world and by their stupidity had
endangered the rest. Munich, he maintained, was the result of
such stupidity, as well as an indication that the Chamberlain
government had failed. Calling for a leader of strength and
integrity to replace it, he pointed out that both Europe and the
Far East demanded qualities that the Chamberlain government
did not possess.

The sharpness of Bromfield's attack drew adverse criticism
from both the left and the right in America and abroad. The
right regarded it as a call to arms against Fascism, and the
left interpreted his demand for a leader as an attempt to use
the means of Fascism in an effort to repel it. Neither side saw
his pamphlet for what it was then and remains: an attempt to
bring Bromfield's personal philosophy, as he had stated it in *The*

Rains Came, to bear on the world crisis. In effect Bromfield was pleading for the emergence of a natural aristocrat with the strength, determination, and integrity of the Maharanee or Hattie Tolliver to take command of the situation and to do what had to be done, regardless of cost. Simultaneously it was his condemnation, as forceful and pointed as he could make it, of those who were dominated by the drive for profits and markets at the expense of traditional human values. Although events were to prove him right and although Winston Churchill was to emerge as the natural leader he sought, the pamphlet engendered cries of oversimplification that did nothing to enhance Bromfield's reputation.

Although *The Rains Came* had been profitably sold to Hollywood, Bromfield's purchase of the farm, his construction of the "Big House," and the needs of the depleted soil left him short of immediate cash. Hollywood once more provided a source, and, although he had sworn that he would never sign a contract as a screenwriter again, he did so with the reservation that he could break the contract when he wanted to. During the fall and winter of 1939-40 he spent much of his time in Hollywood, working on the script for *Brigham Young*—with whom he felt a sentimental kinship after his rediscovery of Pleasant Valley—and acting as a technical advisor for the movie version of *The Rains Came.* But again he was unhappy in Hollywood; he was eager to be working on the farm and telling the story of France to Americans; and he had writing of his own to do. Meanwhile, he assembled a volume of short stories and novellas that had been published in *Cosmopolitan* during the 1930's, and he began work on his second Indian novel, *Night in Bombay.*

IV It Takes All Kinds

Two outstanding characteristics dominate the stories of *It Takes All Kinds:* they are for the most part long and tedious, and they are characterized by a close attention to trivia of incident and setting that robs them of depth and dramatic impact. The first, "McLeod's Folly," is the story of a small-town newspaper's attempt to destroy the corrupt local political machine. Complete with violence, a touch of sex, and an easily resolved love triangle, the novella refuses to explore the many ramifications and various levels inherent in a conflict between good and evil. Instead it depends on unbelievable coincidence, melodrama, and clichés to achieve a predetermined solution.

"Bitter Lotus" and "Better Than Life" are equally inane and almost equally long. "Bitter Lotus" is, as Bromfield comments in a footnote, a "technical experiment" in which he took three characters from *The Rains Came*—Tom Ransome, Lady Esketh, and Lord Esketh—placed them in a different set of circumstances in a different Indian setting, and allowed them "to work out their destinies." In the course of the story Tom Dantry and Lady Groton have an affair; Lord Groton, betrayed both in marriage and in business, dies; and the lovers are driven off into their punishment by a mob of angry Indians. More realistically but certainly less effectively, Bromfield places them in the ranks of the exploiters who destroy lives and values indiscriminately in their pursuit of a fulfillment that they can find only in bed. "Better Than Life" is an insignificant, unbelievable story of a boarding house that remains in modern New York as a remnant of the 1890's and of the futile efforts of a gangster to turn it into a night club.

"New York Legend," "The Girl Who Knew Everybody," "Good Time Bessie," "That Which Never Returns," and "Aunt Flora" are shorter and less tedious but no more profound. In each of them Bromfield attempts to capture a character caught in a set of circumstances, who portrays either the emptiness that inevitably seizes the person who accepts the meaningless values of modern society, or else the nature of the person who rejects those standards in favor of the human values inherent in love and understanding. But in execution trivialities and clichés obscure both the substance and the stylistic merits of the stories. Only in "The Hand of God" does Bromfield overcome most of these shortcomings to create a genuine mood as well as character, but again he depends on a stereotyped, consciously ironic incident to provide the just retribution that his mood and characters make necessary.

As a whole, the collection is an example of technical competence without substance, reiterating the fact that Bromfield's major talent became a deficit in many instances. He writes so well so easily that too often the physical act of putting words on paper overwhelms the artistic impulse that demands control, selectivity, and meaning, as well as form, if the result is to be anything more than second rate.

However, one curious theme recurs in these stories. In almost all of them and most prominently in "The Hand of God" a house plays an important role as a focal point, as a reflection of personality, and as a symbol of permanence in a world of changing values. Here, perhaps, is the key to the lack of meaning in the stories as Bromfield found himself increasingly preoccupied with his search for permanence in his own life; here, too, is the motive inherent in the construction of the "Big House" on Malabar Farm.

V   Night in Bombay

Although *It Takes All Kinds* was no worse than Bromfield's other collections of short fiction, it is unique because it was not followed by a major work. Instead it was followed by *Night in Bombay,* a novel in which Bromfield attempted to use the same thematic structure that he had used in *The Rains Came;* he approaches it, however, through the international society that makes its headquarters in Bombay. The result is neither so sweeping nor so strong as *The Rains Came,* and Bromfield's efforts to end it on the same note of affirmation with which he concluded the earlier novel are both weak and forced. The entire novel has about it an air of hasty craftsmanship rather than directed thought; and this tendency, beginning with *Night in Bombay,* marred his remaining novels. Perhaps the operations of the farm and the demands of his peripheral interests absorbed the energy he had formerly devoted to writing. In any case *Night in Bombay* marks in many ways the end of Louis Bromfield the serious novelist and the emergence of Bromfield as a farmer who indulges in writing as an avocation and as an active, forceful propagandist for a variety of causes.

The novel centers on the activities of the international society that makes its headquarters in the Taj Mahal Hotel, an approach that combines the structure of Vicki Baum's *Grand Hotel* with that of Thornton Wilder's *Bridge of San Luis Rey.* But Bromfield is not willing to allow his plot or his theme to grow out of his collection of characters; rather, he imposes characterization upon plot and theme. The result is an array of weakly presented character sketches superimposed upon a slowly-moving and unreal sequence of events. Both are carefully contrived to reinforce and validate his conclusions about the nature of man and about the choice man is forced to make as the world moves inevitably toward destruction or redemption.

The plot of the novel revolves around the emotional entanglements of three Americans: Bill Wainright, a playboy who is attempting to transcend his weakness of character; Carol Halma, a former beauty queen, born Olga Janssen on a Minnesota farm; and Buck Merrill, who has devoted his life to helping the Indian villagers put new, more productive agricultural techniques into practice. Bill and Buck had been friends as undergraduates at Cornell, and Carol and Bill had been briefly married five years before. Against the background of a wide variety of character types, Bill again falls in love with Carol; but she, seeking meaning and direction in her life, loves Buck, who, in seeking to free himself from a puritan background that threatens to destroy him, reciprocates. In the end Bill gives up Carol and makes it possible for her and Buck to be married so that Buck can go on with his work in the villages.

The plot is both trite and trivial, and so are the demands that Bromfield makes on his characters so that action may work out. Actually the plot is the least important element in the novel, existing only to serve as a convenient framework upon which Bromfield can erect his array of characters, his Indian background, his indignation at the exploiters, and his hatred of puritanism. But the weakness of the plot results in a weak book since it fails to hold the elements together. Many of these elements are as good as any of Bromfield's best work, although little of his old indignation makes itself felt except in anti-puritan expressions that are close to diatribes. But they lack the transmuting element that would combine all these elements into a serious, fully developed novel, and the result is ineffective.

In spite of this basic defect, the novel contains a good deal of evidence to indicate that Bromfield was attempting neither to exploit his Indian material for commercial purposes nor merely, as he later asserted, to write a sort of "notebook" that would include the characters he had met in Bombay so that he would not forget them. Rather it is a serious if hasty and ill-conceived attempt to reinforce his thematic statement in *The Rains Came* by emphasizing a point that had played only a small part in the thematic development of that novel. This belief is that a great many Americans are closer to the old traditions of construction than to exploitation. Consequently their integrity has not yet been completely destroyed by materialism, and they are capable of the selfless dedication demanded by attempts to fulfill human destiny through the extension of human dignity. As a result they can provide the leadership that neither Europe, dominated by materialism and appearance, nor the East, torn between loyalties to the past and dedication to the future, can provide. But first the Americans must purge themselves of the selfish materialism represented by Carol's jewels, the regard for appearance that had brought her the title of Miss Minnesota, and the residue of puritanism that threatens to come between Buck and his dedication to God and nature. Bill Wainright serves as the catalyst by which all three are accomplished.

The weight of this thematic development is carried by the characterizations of Wainright, Merrill, and Carol and by the outcome of the plot. Both elements indicate that each of the three can find within himself the strength and the integrity to make the choice that each must make if the world is to be reconstructed rather than destroyed. However, weakness of characterization and plot detracts from the effectiveness of the theme and makes it appear shallow and devoid of conviction.

Of the three major characters only Carol appears to have any depth other than that which Bromfield states she has. Wainright, in spite of his resolution to reform and to find meaning in his work and despite his helping Buck regain physical and emotional strength, is hopelessly weak. His final attempt at complete honesty in order to save Carol from deportation so that she may marry Buck is not only out of character but almost unbelievable. However, the workings of the plot demand it. Although Merrill is portrayed as being more complex than Wainright, the purging effect of his premarital honeymoon with Carol is equally dubious, and his renewed strength and dedication are as unconvincing as Wainright's sudden and fleeting surge of strength and self-sacrifice.

Carol, however, represents the completely natural woman. Although her beauty has allowed her to be deluded by appearance, in the course of the novel she finds the way through appearance to ultimate spiritual reality. The solid roots of her Minnesota background have preserved her integrity beneath the thin veneer of her superficial beauty and hardness. Only momentarily does she feel that she is purposeless and doomed; then she finds peace in her relationship with Merrill, a relationship that is unrealistically and sentimentally characterized as an act for which all India would be grateful if it could but know. As the symbol of the eternal strength of woman, Carol is sought out by the weak and degenerate, each of whom wants to feed on her strength. But only Merrill, to whom she gives of it freely, is worthy of it; and only he finds the strength that he seeks. Carol, too, emerges as a representation of life as Bromfield would have it rather than as it is. As the kindhearted courtesan she is closely related to his short-story portrayals of bootleggers as nature's noblemen, and she is equally unreal.

The best parts of the novel occur in the background, both in the contrast between the real world of India and the artificial world of the Taj Mahal Hotel and the racetrack, and in the international array of characters who people both worlds. There is no communication between India and the hotel except through the servants who, in order to survive in the real world, have themselves become exploiters by telling lies that are different only in that they are more fantastic and emphasizing appearance that is only less subtle. Those who inhabit the hotel do not see either the struggle of the masses to survive or the meaning of Merrill's work, and they have no concept of the fact that their own struggles for survival are a more sophisticated but no less vicious manifestation of the jungle-like world that they refuse to see. In their concern with appearances they are doomed to frustration, to failure, and to ultimate extinction because they ignore the nature of life.

The secondary characters are more interesting and more believable than the primary characters, but they too are essentially types. These people are drawn from life as Bromfield found them rather than as he would prefer them to be, and the contrast between them and the protagonists is almost startling. All of the westerners and almost all of the easterners are symbolic of the degeneracy and evil that have paralyzed the West—allowing it to be taken over by the exploiters—and that threaten to do the same thing in India. But, significantly, the bulk of the westerners are deported by the governor at the end of the novel.

Among these secondary characters the two most interesting are the Baroness Stefani, a fat, evil woman of vague Middle East origin, who runs a successful chain of high-class European brothels, and Mrs. Stitch Trollope, Australian by birth and condemned by her own weakness to existence on the periphery of international café society. The Baroness, on a talent-scouting trip, is Bromfield's most complete and most successful portrait of evil personified when, with determination and confidence, she makes her plans. She knows that the degeneracy of the West and its feverish pursuit of momentary, sensual pleasures have placed it permanently in her hands, and she is just as certain of her ultimate triumph in the East. Her only miscalculation allows Carol to escape her; she recognizes Carol's type but fails to recognize that her American integrity, hidden by appearance as it is, will not permit her to be bought. But the Baroness, aware that there are many Carols, unperturbably waits for the next.

Her rival for Carol's attention, Mrs. Trollope, represents another aspect of the West: the weakness that reduces it to a parasitic existence feeding on the strength of younger, more vigorous life. In her desperate efforts to survive by gambling, she sees Carol as lucky; after Carol rejects her and she fails in her stupid, desperate attempt to survive by stealing Carol's jewels, she has no alternative but suicide. Both Mrs. Trollope and the Baroness recognize that the only sure means of survival in a hostile world is provided by the security that comes from money; but the Baroness, a wise and strong woman who is the antithesis of Bromfield's conventionally strong women, intuitively recognizes and uses the forces that control a sick world, while Mrs. Trollope, lacking either strength or wisdom, can do no more than clutch desperately at those who are stronger, hoping that they will help her survive.

Among the others in the background of the world of the Taj Mahal Hotel are the Indian counterparts of the Baroness and Mrs. Trollope; they are the Maharajah of Jellapore, more informally known as "Jelly," and Mr. Botlivala, a dissolute Parsee who seeks in his own way to feed on Carol's beauty and strength. Although less sharply drawn than the Baroness and Mrs. Trollope, both men are equally clearly symbolic of the sickness that is threatening to overwhelm the East in spite of the efforts of the builders. "Jelly," like the Baroness, is an evil, intriguing troublemaker; born to be a goodnatured bookmaker, he is forced by circumstance to be "the king of kings, the father and mother of his people." [2] Without either strength or integrity he can find his only escape in the sort of thing represented by the wares the Baroness has placed on the market for a price.

Botlivala, like Mrs. Trollope, is a weak castoff who can only survive by feeding on the strong. But because he is rich, his appetites are satisfied by appearance. When he too is rejected by Carol, his only recourse is to create a scandalous scene; he hopes to destroy her reputation just as Mrs. Trollope had hoped to punish her by stealing her jewels. But he makes a fool of himself because Carol has no need of the artificial props of either money or appearance. Botlivala, like "Jelly," represents the nature of the India that exists for and by exploitation and that can only mock the work Merrill is doing.

In the background, too, but as one who rejects the world of the Taj Mahal Hotel except in the rare instances in which he can use it, is Colonel Moti, the head of the Institute of Tropical Diseases and the friend and admirer of Buck Merrill. As one of the characters who appeared briefly in *The Rains Came*, Moti was characterized as a ruthless destroyer of disease and super-stition. In *Night in Bombay* he comes into clearer focus as a man dedicated to saving humanity and to giving it dignity—so much so that he is willing to use tactics and even people that he despises. His efforts to play God; his denunciation of "the mean, unnatural spirit of Zwingli, of Calvin, of John Knox" [3] that has destroyed the West; and his condemnation of the superstitions that threaten the East, give moments of strength and credibility to the otherwise weak and unconvincing pattern of plot and theme. It is unfortunate that Bromfield did not make Moti a major character.

To account for the weaknesses in this novel is not difficult. As the first product of a period in Bromfield's life in which he had made a major shift more abrupt than any since he had left the farm and the town almost twenty-five years before, it was born of his determination to use once more the Indian mate-rial as well as the conclusions he had drawn from it. At the same time, however, the major part of his attention was focused on the farm, the construction of the "Big House," and the attempt to put into practice the concepts that had long been mere romantic yearnings. He had begun to find real meaning in his closeness to the Ohio countryside.

VI *The Big House*

The building of the "Big House" came to symbolize for Bromfield the permanence of his return to Richland County, his plan to bring the family dream to reality, and his sense of personal identification with the mythological past and the demanding present of the Ohio hill country. Although he did not sever his ties with the successful people with whom he had surrounded himself for most of his adult life, the erection of the "Big House" was to mark his independence of the rootless life that they represented and to be the affirmation of his new allegiance. Using as a basis the clean lines of an old Western Reserve style farmhouse, Bromfield designed a house that reflected the active forcefulness of his own personality. At the same time it was to portray that fusion of Southern opulence and of New England austerity which occurs on the watershed between Lake Erie and the Ohio River. Architecturally the fusion is obvious, and the "Big House" shows it. But the house also commemorates the subject matter of Bromfield's best fiction: the meeting and quarreling of two alien cultures as they merged into a new, peculiarly Midwestern identity. In the house that stands on the hillside as though it had been there forever, Bromfield took the course that was to lead to problems more complex and more evocative of subtleties than he had anticipated when he decided to return.

CHAPTER 6

The Decline of a Novelist

I Wild Is the River

ESTABLISHED in the "Big House," Bromfield was caught
up in the romantic and emotional security of the past and
in the immediate practical problem of applying to his land
scientific agricultural techniques as well as many he had learned
from European peasants. Amid activities that took much of the
energy he had previously put into writing, Bromfield produced
his next novel, *Wild Is the River*. Essentially it is an attempt to
define once more, and for the first time in affirmative terms, that
same quarrel between the Jeffersonian and the Hamiltonian philosophies that had earlier resulted in his being driven from
the land. He had returned in confidence to reclaim the land
that had been exploited by the victors in the past, and the novel,
in spite of its melodrama, reflects the assurance of victory that
he feels. For the setting and the plot of the novel Bromfield
again, as in *Night in Bombay*, made an unfortunate choice. In
character and theme, this novel, too, reveals the same sort of
unconscious manipulation that results in ineffectiveness. But
whereas *Night in Bombay* is merely a weak novel, *Wild Is the
River* is a bad one; and efforts to dismiss it as a lighthearted
effort at sentimental romance ignore the seriousness with which
Bromfield approached it and developed its theme.

The novel is set in New Orleans during the Civil War occupation period under General Benjamin Butler, and a thinly disguised portrait of him is used to give verisimilitude to the
story. Against the background of a war that plays a large role
in the development of the theme of the novel, Bromfield con-
structs a plot complete with multiple love entanglements,

intrigue, passion, and violence enough to justify the novel's wide acceptance as a melodramatic romance. Major Tom Bedloe, a Union officer from New England; Agnes Wicks, his New England fiancée; and Hector MacTavish, a dedicated young planter-guerilla, provide the basis for the love entanglement. It is further complicated by the love of La Lionne—the madam of an exclusive brothel that degenerates under the occupation—for Tom and by his infatuation with the Baroness de Leche, a witch-like member of an aristocratic Creole family. In the end Tom is shot by La Lionne, who escapes to France on the same ship that carries the Baroness to her spiritual home in Paris; then Agnes and Hector determine to seek a new life in the new country of the West.

Although the plot structure has much in common with that of *Night in Bombay,* with an additional injection of sex and violence, actually the interwoven subplots, including the adventures of Agnes and her Aunt Tam on their way to New Orleans; the love affair between Agnes' brother, the virginal New England poet, Lieutenant David Wicks, and the innocent prostitute, Clelis; the activities of the Confederate guerillas; and the antics of General Wicks and his wife as insensitive exploiters provide more complexity than appears in *Night in Bombay.* In fact these subjects strain to the breaking point the willing suspension of belief that is necessary for enjoyment of a historical novel.

Although the basic plot is so stereotyped that it is hackneyed, it, like the subplots, is designed to permit the development of Bromfield's theme, which asserts that the natural aristocrats of Jeffersonianism will, through strength and integrity, survive and triumph while the exploiting Hamiltonians are destroyed. The Civil War has long been regarded by some historians as the climax of that battle, and Bromfield accepts that interpretation almost wholeheartedly. But, in its formulation as well as its specific illustration in this novel, the interpretation demands a loose, oversimplified, and often distorted or biased interpretation of historic facts and personalities.

In attempting to make vivid the contrasts between the two warring philosophies, Bromfield uses characters, setting, plot, and interpretation of historical fact in whatever proportions are necessary as the theme unfolds. The result damages the novel beyond salvage as a work of fiction, at the same time making it totally unreliable as history. However, Bromfield manages to dispose of the factors that complicate the simple unraveling of his thematic development with disarming simplicity that is so naïve as to be almost amusing. The implications that he ignores are among the most significant elements in any attempt to understand or interpret the American past.

In characterization Bromfield attempts to define clearly each of the many types that play a role in the battle, labeling them so definitely that they exist exclusively as symbols, as he had done in *Night in Bombay*. As a result none of the characters in this novel is either believable or acceptable, even as evidence for the validity of Bromfield's theme. As the extreme factions of the two philosophies, he uses General Wicks and Hector Mac-Tavish. Wicks, drawn on General Butler, is the "Spoon Stealer" who has come to New Orleans to impose his puritan philosophy on the defeated town and to enrich himself in the process. Accepting the stereotyped distortions of the Southern interpretation of the occupation, Bromfield commits his most serious offense against historic fact as he ignores Butler's commendable if stern performance that gave New Orleans its first efficient civil administration and almost eliminated its perennial disease problem as well. Instead he portrays Wicks as the same New England shopkeeper who had despoiled the Ohio countryside and who has found an opportunity for corruption on a much grander scale. Wicks's removal by Lincoln, actually in Butler's case dictated by political and foreign policy necessities, Bromfield sees as the recognition of Wicks's innate dishonesty by the simple, rustic, honest Abraham Lincoln. The demands of the plot dictate such distortions, but it is inexcusable to employ them because they insult Butler's reputation and propagate a misinterpretation that should be eliminated by objective analysis.

Just as Wicks is cast in the role of villain, Hector MacTavish is cast as the hero. As totally and recognizably pure as Wicks is evil, MacTavish is not one of the old Creole aristocrats whom Bromfield pictures as physically and morally decadent; he is the son of a Scotch immigrant who had come to build up the South rather than to exploit it as the hereditary aristocrats had done. Recognizing both the evil of the shopkeeper philosophy and the degeneracy of the Old South, MacTavish is a builder by nature, who dislikes slavery and the "bad niggers" while he loves the land and the "good niggers." Through his good influence Aunt Tam rejects the puritan background that had dominated her in spite of her hatred for it, Agnes grows up to have faith in MacTavish and his dreams, and all of them, together with the "good niggers," go off to build in the West.

Tom Bedloe, who first appears in the novel as an anachronistic individual who doesn't quite fit as the theme unfolds, is the most interesting and the most complex character. A New England scion who is wild and different, he is earthy, sensuous, and as attractive to women as he is attracted to the degenerate South. But because he rejects his New England background, he does not bridge the two cultures. A character full of possibilities for development, as Bromfield recognizes early in the novel, he is rejected in favor of the more tractable MacTavish, first by imprisonment and then by murder in order to resolve the plot. The resulting defect in structure as well as character development indicates that Bromfield had such serious intentions that he was unable to handle them easily. Moreover, the sudden emergence of MacTavish as Bedloe's replacement indicates the haste and carelessness with which Bromfield wrote the novel and also his determination to ignore the subtleties of his theme.

In Agnes and David, Bromfield furthers his use of character evidence by introducing them as innocent, malleable, and perceptive; they are destined either to spiritual destruction by the rigid puritanism and shoddy values of New England or to fulfillment through the discovery of their own inner strength and integrity. But free from the New England environment and introduced to persons who have preserved and extended personal integrity, each of them recognizes true human values and finds fulfillment. For Agnes both discovery and attainment come readily in spite of the long, perilous, and ridiculous journey that Bromfield sends her through; she simply has to follow her love. But David's situation is infinitely more complex, so the dilemma is solved by the convenience of yellow fever. Bromfield's implication, of course, is that his natural aristocrats may arise anywhere and that environment is not inescapable. But the concept is lost in the oversimplification and melodrama in which it is clothed.

In his secondary characters, as well as in setting and background, Bromfield carries through this oversimplification. Aunt Tam, who is projected as one of Bromfield's strong, determined women, actually emerges as a caricature of one, as she rejects the New England of Mr. Emerson, Mr. Holmes, and her shopkeeping ancestry. She merely demands that the world be turned over to the natural aristocracy represented by MacTavish and her young niece. Although Bromfield had intended the long journey from Cuba by way of a wretched Spanish ship and the Delta Swamp country to New Orleans as the opportunity for Aunt Tam's natural strength to exhibit itself and for Agnes to gain maturity, the exaggerated melodrama of both the trip and Aunt Tam's determination to experience everything there is to be experienced make the entire adventure tedious, ridiculous, and extraneous.

The young Baroness, like Bedloe, has the potential of being an interesting and complex character. She exhibits subtleties and paradoxes that, if explored, might provide insight into the many-leveled ramifications of social upheaval. But again, after preparing carefully for such exploration, Bromfield is content to over-simplify her as a symbol of the decadent aristocracy of Southern exploiters who had brought down ruin upon the country as he turns to a simple, one-level explanation that his theme demands. Had he explored both Bedloe and the Baroness as it is evident he had intended to do, undoubtedly the result would have been more satisfactory.

In the background Bromfield contrasts New England austerity with the opulence of the Creole South as further documentary evidence that both are destructive to agrarian and human values, and the countless background characters are drawn in the same image. All Northern soldiers are drunken, savage exploiters; and all Southern citizens, black and white, are victims of degeneracy and superstition—except, of course, for the occasional natural aristocrat who may emerge from any of the groups to go, in the end, to the new country of the West with the noble MacTavish and the good Agnes.

Bromfield's literary technique is unacceptable in the novel, and his oversimplified interpretation of the meaning of the Civil War is a distortion that reduces to meaninglessness the war that in so many ways epitomizes the American tragedy. In reducing it to a quarrel between farmers and shopkeepers, he completely ignores its key position in the continuing American revolution that had been successfully pressing for the expansion of the dignity of the individual in American life. In Bromfield's dis-torted view the majority is without dignity and undeserving, and the men who sacrificed safety for principle are reduced to the level of spoon-stealers, lechers, and destroyers of the American ideal.

The plot, characterizations, and background are parodies of those in *Night in Bombay* exaggerated to the point where their weaknesses become grotesque. At the same time they combine to make a clear, positive statement of Bromfield's own position at the time. *Wild Is the River* is Bromfield's symbolic rejection of the life he had been leading both 'in America and abroad, caught between the exploiting worlds of decadence and commercialism; and it is the declaration of his determination to turn to building. Just as MacTavish was determined to found a simple, self-sufficient society in the West, so Bromfield was determined to do the same thing at "Malabar Farm." But such convictions, no matter how strong, are not enough to provide the substance for an acceptable novel—as *Wild Is the River* bears testimony. Unfortunately, however, the novel was not to be a momentary lapse. Instead it is the first of a series of novels in which everything is subordinated to the expression of a single, simple point of view at the expense of literary achievement.

By the time *Wild Is the River* was published, Bromfield had moved beyond the planning stage at "Malabar Farm" and was actively engaged in farming on a cooperative plan that was designed to give each family residing there an adequate living and a share of the profits after Bromfield had received a fair return on his investment. The farm community was to be as nearly self-sufficient as possible, purchasing nothing that could be raised on the farm itself. In results, although not in equipment and techniques, the farm was to provide evidence that the dream of Jefferson and of the old Colonel was both possible and practicable in the twentieth century. As head of the community Bromfield began to see himself as a true son of The Enlightenment, combining the roles of farmer, philosopher, economist, political scientist, and author. Inevitably the roles were to fuse, to the detriment of his talents as a novelist, although the combination was to produce, in such works of nonfiction as *Pleasant Valley*, some of his best as well as his most deeply and genuinely felt writing.

II Until the Day Break

At the same time that he was beginning to regard himself as a practical dirt farmer who was a writer only by avocation,

Bromfield began a novel that was designed to tell the story of France to those Americans whom he was unable to reach during his speaking tours. But the result, *Until the Day Break,* published in the dark days after Pearl Harbor, was neither the story of the French people nor of the tragedy between the wars. Conceived as a message of hope and as a tribute to courage and defiance, in execution it is one of the most outspoken condemnations of an entire people that has ever been produced by a prominent American writer. As a novel, *Until the Day Break* is insignificant; as a piece of propaganda designed to arouse hatred, it is outstanding. Like *Wild Is the River* it is so clearly a statement of deep conviction that it is a masterpiece of oversimplification, distortion, and condemnatory generalization.

Until the Day Break is set in Paris during the first year of the German occupation. The trivial plot describes the underground activities of Roxana Dawn, an American show girl born Irma Peters in Indiana; her lover Nicky, a Russian refugee from World War I; her manager, d'Absizzi, a Middle Easterner of vague ancestry; and a motley crew of foreigners who love France. This international group is reinforced by an occasional Frenchman. In the novel Roxie plays Mata Hari to a degenerate, sentimental German major, while the others publish annoying newspapers and kill an occasional German. Finally, when Nicky is killed, Roxie, emulating Poe, lures the German to her wine cellar, where she locks him in to die.

Characterization is as trivial as the plot. Roxie is an anemic Carol Halma; the others, including the German major, are symbols of the appropriate virtues and vices. Although Bromfield uses plot and character to substantiate the theory of society he had advanced in *England, A Dying Oligarchy* and to illustrate the germination of the new society of responsibility and integrity that would prevail after the exploiters had mutually destroyed each other, all these elements are subservient to a constant cry of hatred and condemnation of the Germans and of all things German. Not Major Kurt von Wessellhoft, not Hitler, not Nazism are the villains of the novel; they are merely symptomatic of the sickness that is the German people.

All the elements in the German character that, in Bromfield's view, make it what it is are exemplified in Major von Wessellhoft. Were it not for his role as the symptom of total human depravity that is Germany, the portrayal of the major would have been a masterpiece of degeneracy. Proud, scheming, resentful, and sexually degenerate, von Wessellhoft is the personification of the German sickness that has contaminated Europe. In spite of lip service to the part played by the French and English politicians in France's downfall and perfunctory comments about the universality of guilt, the novel is an overwhelming indictment of the people whom Bromfield epitomizes in the major: the "dull and pompous and muddled and sentimental and brutal"[1] Germans, a people of bad taste, bad food, gross appetites, revolting emotionalism, and vicious self-deception.

Perhaps the most realistic and perceptive comments in the book are Bromfield's attempts to define the nature of hate and the peculiar nature of refugees to feel it with an intensity almost impossible to an American. But these few rare instances are far from enough to redeem the book. Although it merits the oblivion to which it has been consigned and will undoubtedly retain, nevertheless the book should not be forgotten. Rather, like the incidents that engendered it and the spectre of the gas ovens and concentration camps, it should be revived periodically to document the bestiality of men and the depths of emotion to which they descend when reason is overwhelmed. As a reminder of an episode that one would prefer to forget—but does so only if one wishes to repeat it—the book is invaluable; but for the sake of Bromfield's literary reputation it would have been better had it never been written.

III   Mrs. Parkington

Bromfield knew that the criticism directed at his last four books was justified, that all of his writing after *The Rains Came* was weak when it was not downright bad. But he was also aware of the reasons for his seeming inability to write anything substantial: he had been employing his genuine gifts for character development and storytelling merely to disseminate points of view on many things, and he had turned to unfamiliar subject matter in order to provide the means of dissemination. In his next novel he determined to return to his old, successful subject matter and technique, to let personal philosophic expression grow out of his story and his people. The result was *Mrs. Parkington,* a novel that ranks in stature just below his best work of the 1920's and early 1930's. It is both his most carefully controlled novel and his best in technical execution.

In *Mrs. Parkington* Bromfield uses as a basis the character of a strong and noble woman, the New York dowager-socialite Mrs. Susie Parkington. As the novel opens Mrs. Parkington, at eighty-four, is the head of her family and its only source of strength. In the course of the novel Bromfield takes Mrs. Parkington through three major crises that threaten her family during the next several months, and he also re-creates the long, eventful, and crisis-laden life that had taken her from a cheap boarding house in Leaping Rock, Nevada, to Fifth Avenue; had made her the woman that she is; and had given her strength and wisdom to match her integrity. The result is the ideal portrait of the strong woman that Bromfield had been working toward from the beginning of his writing.

Essentially the novel explores in depth both the concept of the natural aristocracy and the nature of the degenerate destroyers who threaten human values and pervert human decency. However, for the first time Bromfield recognizes the complexity of the conflict; and rather than evade it as he had done in the last three novels, he faces it and provides an answer that is nearly acceptable. In *Mrs. Parkington* Bromfield writes with perspective and objectivity rather than indignation or emotion; as a result, the novel is a carefully controlled statement of belief as well as Bromfield's last significant work of fiction. Mrs. Parkington's transition from Leaping Rock to Park Avenue is merely a symbolic representation of her escape from a grim, overwhelming reality to mature wisdom—just what Bromfield had attempted to portray so many times before. But here he is almost completely successful both because Mrs. Parkington is his most fully realized character and because he shows a new and deeper understanding of the people who surround her, of the America that had produced them, and of Mrs. Parkington herself.

The three crises with which Mrs. Parkington is faced at the age of eighty-four are in her immediate family: her daughter Alice, once a duchess, dies after an empty life; her great-granddaughter Janie determines to marry a nobody in spite of her parents' wishes; and her grandson-in-law Amory Stilham has gambled with and lost the securities he had been entrusted with as a broker. As the novel develops, Mrs. Parkington comes to understand these crises and to provide the strength necessary to solve them or to accept their insolvability in the light of the wisdom that her integrity has allowed her to accumulate over the years.

At eighty-four Mrs. Parkington's strength manifests itself in wisdom, in integrity, and—most importantly—in innocence, a quality that Bromfield had never before seen as necessary to the natural aristocrat. But it is an innate rather than an acquired characteristic; consequently, it had ensnared Major Augustus Parkington, the speculator, into marriage back in Leaping Rock when he had only planned to make her his mistress, and it had preserved her from the corruption that comes from having too much money without a proper sense of values to guide its use. Throughout the Major's manipulations and conspicuous consumption, in spite of his unscrupulous use of money and power to smash those who opposed or refused to accept them, and even through the Major's many affairs and a brief one of her own, Mrs. Parkington's innocence has preserved her from the corruption that struck down her own children and grandchildren. Among her family only her great-granddaughter Janie, who has the integrity and innocence that had passed over two generations, is preserved from corruption.

The most important aspect of this quality of innocence is its source as a free gift from God and nature. Because it is not acquired but innate, Bromfield no longer condemns the people who lack it. Instead he exhibits a compassion for their shortcomings that eliminates his old indignation and, more importantly, enhances their depth and believability as individuals. At the same time this new recognition contributes to the credibility of his strong protagonist as he emphasizes her belief that those who receive special gifts must accept the responsibility that goes with them and must love those who are weaker, not because they are weak but because they are less fortunate and perhaps more human.

As a result of her insight into the nature of her gift, Mrs. Parkington gives freely of the strength that she has, permitting her daughter to die with a measure of dignity that had eluded her in life, aiding Janie to marry the young man who is a good man rather than a good catch, and making a legally unnecessary but morally obligatory restitution for Amory's crime. At the same time she recognizes that she cannot save others from the effects of their weaknesses any more than she can prevent them from being weak. She can only attempt to soften the results. So intensely does she feel the necessity to protect people from the effects of their weakness that three times in her life she deliberately violated her integrity in order to save others from pain: in her brief youthful affair with a young man; in blackmailing the Duke in order to save Alice from a scandalous contested divorce; and in her willingness to bribe in Amory's case in order to avoid the scandal that threatened to prevent Janie's marriage. Instead of destroying her integrity, these lapses reinforce it, as they point out the lengths to which she is willing to go in order to accept the responsibility that her strength demands of her.

At the same time that Mrs. Parkington meets her current crises, she is forced back in time both to the situations and to the people who made them inevitable. The resulting skillfully handled flashbacks provide remarkable portraits both of individuals, especially Major Parkington, and of the country and the values that made the robber barons possible. The Major emerges as a fully drawn character that contrasts strongly with Mrs. Parkington; he is a likable scoundrel who reveals the qualities that Bromfield had attempted but failed to convey in his portrayal of Pierre Radier in *A Modern Hero*.

As Mrs. Parkington realizes, the Major and the last half of the nineteenth century were made for each other. Strong, boisterous, forceful, ambitious, shrewd, ruthless, and sensual, Gus mirrored his times as a robber baron who exploited his country relentlessly at the same time that he gave it much of his strength in return. Selfish and unscrupulous, the Major is also magnificently alive. The product of a violent age, he lives in the glory of violence and dies seeking it rather than the peace that would have destroyed him. As he lives in her memory, Mrs. Parkington also retains the vividness of her ambiguous feeling for him: a profound love for his strength, determination, and wit; a deep contempt for the means and ends in which he employed them. She recognizes that, in an age of builders rather than of exploiters, he would have been in prison where he belonged; and he surely would have been as the New Deal attempted to rebuild the America that had come close to destruction at the hands of the Major and his friends.

In her recall of the Major and his times, Mrs. Parkington deepens her understanding of them as she sees their relationship to the crises that she now faces. The money and power that her husband grasped so eagerly had destroyed her sons and her daughter: the boys, because their energy was devoted to pleasure that was overtly approved by the Major; Alice, because she was forced into a position that demanded a strength she did not possess. In each case the destruction was wrought by the money that only she knew had a great potential for evil rather than the fulfillment that the Major found in the power that it provides, the sons saw in the momentary physical pleasures it could buy, and Alice sought in a marriage that would presumably compensate for the lack of distinction in her own personality. Although Mrs. Parkington knew that these misconceptions would inevitably lead to destruction, dominated by Gus, there was nothing she could do except wait for the inevitable.

Mrs. Parkington recognizes, too, the closeness of the relationship between Gus's time and the present. Just as she is still attempting to make order out of the emotional chaos resulting from her husband's drive for power and prestige, America was trying in the 1930's to bring order out of the economic chaos that the robber barons had caused. In attempting to do so, the government has imposed itself between the exploiters and the people; and Amory, whose activities are neither venturesome nor sporting—as were the Major's—but merely stupid, is caught as a result. The Major had been a reflection of his era and had understood its rules; Amory cannot understand that the new era will not tolerate his greed and ambition nor that it cannot be dismissed contemptuously with the epithet "Red," as he attempts to do.

But a major difference appears between Amory's victims and the Major's and it serves effectively to point out the difference between the men and their values. Gus enriches his friends and destroys his enemies; Amory robs his friends and even his weak, pathetic mistress in his drive for wealth and power. Because Janie's young man, a government attorney, is largely responsible for his detection, Amory is convinced that the young man is a "Red" who is out to smash both the old economic order and the social system based on prestige and power in which Amory believes.

Mrs. Parkington is contemptuous of Amory and of the superficial values that have made his character possible and that have destroyed all of her family except Janie. But she recognizes a number of factors in the world about her that give her confidence in the future: the Major's younger brother Henry, who had refused to be seduced by wealth, is still on the upstate farm and, in his seventies, is still producing sturdy, self-confident children, while her old admirer Lord Haxton, one of those who made Munich possible, is old and afraid; Janie and Ned reject her money as they look confidently into the future; and in the background the war that is sweeping across Europe is destroying forever the world of privilege. In the end, as Mrs. Parkington plans a visit to the ruins of Leaping Rock, she knows too that she is moving into a future that will demand the same kind of strength she has needed for sixty years.

In selecting Mrs. Parkington for his central character, Bromfield eliminated the indignation, hatred, and disgust that had ruined his recent novels; and he gave the novel a wise and convincing restraint new to his work. Although it bears a close relationship in structure and theme to *Twenty-Four Hours, Mrs. Parkington* is greatly superior because Bromfield shows his protagonist in her rise above the destructive influences of great wealth rather than merely implies that it is done—as he had in the earlier novel. As a result, the symbolic return at the end is not an indication of an implied triumphant and sudden victory as the protagonist approaches fulfillment. Bromfield realized by this time that such an ending is nonsense, and the character of Mrs. Parkington makes such an implication impossible. The resulting conclusion is an honest affirmation of faith in a difficult world rather than the assertion of complete victory implicit in *Wild Is the River* and in other products of wishful thinking.

The novel marks, too, a return to Bromfield's earlier stylistic strength. The forced, stilted speeches, the awkward diction, and the unnatural rhetorical flourishes that had begun in *Night in Bombay* and had dominated *Wild Is the River* have disappeared with his indignation. Important also—and undoubtedly contributing to the novel's strength—is its biographical basis, as Ellen Bromfield Geld points out. Mrs. Parkington is an accurate portrayal of Mary Bromfield's Aunt Julia, a woman who had rejected the decadent New England aristocracy out of which she came and who had also provided the strength that a weak family needed. The portrait in the novel is an effective testimonial to Bromfield's admiration for her as well as for the natural aristocracy in which he believed and of which Mrs. Parkington is clearly a member.

As a portrait of America under the New Deal, the book provides a clearer understanding of the phenomenon than any Bromfield had revealed before. The period was not the millennium that so many, including Bromfield, hoped it would be or that many insisted it was. Significantly Bromfield portrays it as a time in which an indignant people, led by an indignant man, rose in righteous anger against those who used power and prestige to exploit them. In their determination to prevent such things from happening again, they were not carrying on a social or economic revolution; they were merely reasserting the democratic heritage that was rightfully theirs. The New Deal, as Bromfield portrays it in the novel, was not a revolutionary or radical movement; it was a conservative movement that looked back to the principles on which he believed America had been founded. The interpretation is interesting, especially because it has been almost lost in the heat of partisan debate, and it is only now being examined by younger historians who see the period in perspective.

The novel implies an approval of the New Deal that Bromfield no longer actually felt. As one of a long line of Democrats, he supported Roosevelt in 1932 and 1936; and the support continued almost until 1940. However, he was increasingly aware that the New Deal was a Jacksonian movement, in which the people placed in trust more of their power in the hands of the government; it was not a Jeffersonian movement that returned power to the people. Unable to see that the ends are the same but that, in an age of greatly concentrated power and wealth in the hands of a few, the people had to meet power with power, Bromfield's misgivings increased. But because the movement fought the industrial oligarchy that he hated, he continued to support it albeit with decreasing enthusiasm. By 1940, however, he was a farmer, and the increasing governmental control of agricultural production seemed to him to be threatening his dream of a self-sustaining agricultural community. The beginning of his long war with big government dates from this period, and this battle led to accusations that Bromfield became reactionary as well as commercial—charges that ignore the consistency with which he sought a Jeffersonian ideal that had become impossible in the twentieth century.

Mrs. Parkington marks the high point of Bromfield's alliance with the New Deal, it is the last of his good novels, and it is the brightest spot in a sequence of second- and third-rate fiction that continued to appear at less frequent intervals until 1951. Had it been written earlier, perhaps after *Twenty-Four Hours,* it might have done much to redeem his reputation among critics, as a sign of further promise and development. But it was too late for that, and, although he was becoming less interested in fiction as a means of expression except in the manner that could only produce bad novels, he continued to write it. In fact, he turned more frequently to magazine articles in which he could express his convictions with a clarity and a force that he knew could only result in bad fiction. In 1943 and 1944, while working on *What Became of Anna Bolton,* he began publishing such articles frequently, turning to his convictions about farming, to his opposition to governmental policies, and to the legendary background of Richland County for his subject matter. The first is primarily of technical interest, the second can attract only economic and political historians, but the third provides an introduction to the most significant literary contribution that he was to make from "Malabar Farm."

IV   What Became of Anna Bolton

After *Mrs. Parkington* Bromfield returned to the war as the background for his next novel. *What Became of Anna Bolton* is another attempt to interpret that war in terms of his belief that it was a purging from which only those with strength, dedication, integrity, and faith would survive. But, although it conveys little of the hatred and indignation of *Until the Day Break,* it also conveys little of the strength of conviction that he was reserving for his nonfiction—just as it contains none of the credibility of *Mrs. Parkington. What Became of Anna Bolton* is, like *Night In Bombay,* not a bad novel; it is merely so incredibly weak that it is insignificant. It was certainly not deserving of the attention that Edmund Wilson gave it when he used it as the basis of a strong attack on Bromfield in his review "What Became of Louis Bromfield."

Anna Bolton is a poor girl from the riverfront of Lewisburg, Ohio. She survives a tragic marriage; then remarries a wealthy inventor; and, after an empty international life, finds meaning and love during the German invasion and occupation of France. The framework of the plot is, while simple and shallow, not impossible to flesh out into an acceptable reaffirmation of the concept of natural aristocracy and the search for fulfillment of the romantic idealist; but the novel, lacking the conviction as well as the insights of *Mrs. Parkington,* remains almost entirely on the level that its plot outline indicates. Perhaps Bromfield had in mind the fleshing out of his characters through the well-rounded contours of Ann Sheridan and the broad shoulders of Charles Boyer, as Wilson maintains; but the more obvious reason for the novel's weakness lies in the narrative technique Bromfield has chosen.

The novel is told from the point of view of a newspaper correspondent who had known Anna in childhood, and the story remains on the level of newspaper reporting. Although there are some vividly described scenes, the most believable of which is the Lewisburg setting, characterization is a matter of black and white sketches, often handled in a mere phrase that contains nothing of life or credibility. The observer records, too, the drama of Anna's search in the way that a Sunday supplement finds appropriate, with melodrama and sentimentality rather than with the depth, restraint, and dignity that human crisis demands. The lack of conviction with which his characters are portrayed is further evidence that for Bromfield fiction no longer had meaning. It was entertainment; it was pragmatic expression, and nothing more. *Mrs. Parkington* was evidence that Bromfield could still write, but *What Became of Anna Bolton* indicates that he no longer had either the interest or the convictions that he had had for so long.

V The World We Live In

Nevertheless several of the novellas that appear in his next book, *The World We Live In,* are among his best shorter fiction. Largely written while he was working on *Mrs. Parkington,* the collection is uneven, and many of the stories lack conviction. But two are both well constructed and believable. Published in late 1944, the collection is made up of stories from *Cosmopolitan.* For the most part, they draw their inspiration from the war, but in one important aspect they show the new sense of fulfillment that he had found in Ohio.

Among the stories in the collection are two that are bad, two that are weak, and five that are better than the short fiction Bromfield had written in the past. The two bad stories, "The Pond" and "True Love," are failures both in concept and in execution. The first, the story of a navy pilot whose death in the war is mystically linked to the reappearance of a farm pond his father had drained, might have provided the basis for a study of the will to destroy the nonutilitarian and the beautiful that seems at the heart of much American farming practice. Instead, Bromfield cloaks commonplace people and a lack of knowledge of naval procedures with a sentimental mysticism. "True Love," the story of a stage electrician's love for an unsuccessful actress with buck teeth, is equally pointless and banal. Both of the stories are also stylistically bad; as in *Wild Is the River,* Bromfield's attempt to recreate diction with which he is unfamiliar is pathetically unreal.

Among the weak stories is "The Man Who Was in Love With Death." A cloak and dagger story, it has as its basis an interesting twist that proves ultimately unsatisfactory although Bromfield maintains a tense pace. This story, too, has a potential for exploring the nature of duty that so often dominates human motivation, but Bromfield loses control of his art for the sake of the twist. In "Thou Shalt Not Covet," a rambling story of Switzerland just before the Nazis came to power, Bromfield provides his atonement for the blanket condemnation of Germany that appeared in *Until the Day Break.* He portrays the Nazis in vivid bestial detail, but, unfortunately, his good Germans remain shadows that eventually go down to a dim and unfelt destruction.

However, in most of the remaining stories Bromfield comes closer to true dramatic incident rather than melodrama, undoubtedly because in almost every case he is retracing material with which he is intimately familiar and because he conceives of them as something more than mere entertainment or linguistic or mechanical exercises. Each of the others deals, too, with an aspect of life about which Bromfield has deep convictions. The results, while well below the level of his best novels, mark an advance over his earlier stories.

"Death in Monte Carlo" and "The Great Façade" are stronger stories than the four already discussed primarily because in them Bromfield emphasizes character revelation and development rather than plot; and he does not distort his people to fit pre-conceived ends. In "Death in Monte Carlo" he portrays the wealthy expatriate women who wander from one fashionable place to another; in "The Great Façade" he depicts the peculiar American type known as the phony, who so often dominates the political scene and even, upon occasion, occupies the White House. "Death in Monte Carlo" is a study in contrasts between two women, Mrs. Pulsifer—a Mrs. Parkington type—and the Princess d'Orobelli, who played a prominent part in *The Strange Case of Miss Annie Spragg*. Both are swept up in the German and Italian assault on France. Mrs. Pulsifer exhausts herself aiding refugees, while the Princess schemes to get her jewels out of Italy. Both reach Monte Carlo, where Mrs. Pulsifer dies of exhaustion and where the Princess saves her jewels at the cost of a life. Alone, she recognizes that she faces a grimmer death in life as her carefully preserved beauty disappears under the strain; and nothing remains for her to do but polish her jewels.

"The Great Façade" is another treatment of much the same theme. It is the story of two men, one who, like Warren G. Harding, looked to be every inch a President, and the other his friend, a brilliant and pathetic cripple who seeks vicarious political power through manipulating that magnificent façade. The ultimate failure is inevitable and ironic; a fool can never be more than what he is, and the ultimate destruction of the façade and his career stems from his friend's recognition of that fact.

The best stories in the collection, and they are two of the best that Bromfield was ever to write, find their inspiration in the integrity and dedication of lonely women who, threatened by war, choose to remain faithful to traditions much older than themselves. "The Old House" has its setting on an island off the southeastern coast of England in a house, built upon Roman foundations, that is slowly losing its battle with the sea in spite of its strength and almost human resistance. In it lives Mrs. Linton, an aging and impoverished relic of a time when England was ruled by adventurous men rather than by shopkeepers. In her own way she reflects the resistance of the house, for she resists governmental as well as social forces that attempt to move her inland. In the end she sacrifices both the house and herself to destroy a German raiding party.

The story incorporates many of the themes of Bromfield's best work: the concept of the strong woman; the belief in the new generation of natural aristocrats and builders who will eventually wrest control from these aging and unimaginative exploiters who have brought on the war; the permanent values inherent in strength, dedication, and integrity; and the regard for a time in the past when men were convinced that they were building a better and more human world and were willing to make the sacrifices their dreams demanded. There is the essence of a dozen novels in this short story, and yet it is so tightly constructed, so dominated by the twin characters of Mrs. Linton and the house that even the melodramatic denouement is acceptable. It is not a perfect story; coincidence as well as the stereotyped German officer mar it. But it is one of the few short stories in which Bromfield has probed beneath the surface of life, and the result is more than his usual technical exercise.

"Daughters of Mars" is almost equally well done, and its subject matter, so improbable that it becomes both believable and acceptable, makes it unique in the Bromfield canon. Four old ladies, daughters of a romantic Southern officer who had resolved never to return to the United States after Appomattox, are faced with life in occupied France. The dignity with which they meet the situation in terms of what Papa would have said, the pathetic trivia of their lives, and the determination with which they give meaning to a vanished and often fraudulent tradition repeat in a lower key the sense of values that dominated Mrs. Linton in her old house that had seen so much triumph and tragedy.

"Up Ferguson Way" is not well executed technically; Bromfield meanders too loosely to achieve the control necessary to the short-story form, but it is significant both for the uniqueness of the subject matter in this collection and because it points out the direction that his worth-while work of the future was to take. Using as a basis the story of Zenobia Ferguson—it had appeared several times in various forms as local color in his earlier novels—Bromfield attempts to elevate it to the realm of folklore by using it to epitomize both the spirit that had built the Ohio country and the peculiar mystique that he finds in this region. Although not an agricultural story, its relationship to *The Farm* and to the mystic passages of *The Strange Case of Miss Annie Spragg* is unmistakable. In many ways it rejects the dedication that successful farming demands, but it also makes clear the sense of identity with nature that Bromfield rediscovered in his return to Richland County.

The publication of *The World We Live In* in 1944 marks, in a way, the end of Bromfield's career as a writer of fiction. He was to write, however, four more volumes, a thin collection of three stories, *Kenny;* and three novels, *Colorado, The Wild Country,* and *Mr. Smith.* By 1945 he recognized that for all practical purposes he was no longer a storyteller, except by occasional avocation. Farming, now his dominant interest, accounted for much of the writing he was to do in the last twelve years of his life; and the meaning of the Ohio country, as he had tried to probe it in "Up Ferguson Way," was his secondary interest. During these last years he wrote seven volumes of nonfiction in which he spent the force and conviction that once went into his novels. Consequently, the last works of fiction remain for the most part on the level that had been reached with *Night In Bombay* and that was only briefly surpassed by *Mrs. Parkington* and the few stories.

VI Kenny

In *Kenny,* Bromfield combines three stories, "Kenny," "Retread," and "The End of the Road"—all of them slight and unimportant. Published in 1947 after a lapse of three years since his last fiction, the collection contains nothing of permanent value. All three stories reflect the war in the background, and "Kenny" draws heavily on Bromfield's sense of identification with the lushness and wildness of nature in the Ohio hill country. "Kenny" is the story of an orphan boy who emerges from the "jungle" of the farm and makes his home there. Possessed of the same mystic sense of identification with living things that marks one who is "teched" by nature, he grows into a half-wild young manhood and marries the daughter of a man and woman who had turned up on the farm years before and who are also "teched." He goes to war almost immediately after his marriage; and, during a night that is bright, moonlit, and mysterious on the farm, he is blown to bits on the other side of the world. Later his Marine Corps buddy, another "teched" one, turns up at the farm and marries Kenny's widow. They have a child who is the image of Kenny in spite of this genetic impossibility.

The story, marked by a consciously contrived mysticism, is hopelessly sentimental. Its only significance lies in the fact that it does represent one of Bromfield's attempts to portray in fiction the completeness with which he identified himself with the Ohio country—an effort that, like its other short-story counterparts, was a failure. Only in the nonfiction of his last years, in which he approaches understanding of his feeling in terms of the folklore of the valley or in his only long attempt to fuse mysticism and folklore in the novel *The Wild Country,* was he to convey his reaction successfully.

"Retread" describes a middle-aged World War I veteran's attempt to recapture his youth by securing an army commission in World War II and by returning to the French village where he first fell in love. Like the character in *The Man Who Had Everything,* he finds that his old love is middle-aged, that he has a strapping son, and that too many things have happened to make either return or understanding possible.

The last story, "The End of the Road," tells of the vicious but just retribution that comes to French collaborators. Told against the sharp contrast between the feverishly gay and unreal prewar international world and the solid reality of the Ohio farmhouse, this narrative is as barbed and vigorous as Bromfield's other condemnations of those who made the war possible. However, in the final rendering of justice, Bromfield withholds judgment; he lets the facts of Mussolini's execution in the Milan public square and that of the Nazi leaders in the courtyard at Nuremberg speak for themselves. This story, like the other two, is marked by two major weaknesses: a slight plot that depends on coincidence and unreal incidents for its movement and an almost total lack of depth and believability in its treatment of characters. But the force with which Bromfield wrote gives it an air of significance that the others lack.

VII Colorado

Bromfield followed *Kenny* with a full-length novel, *Colorado,* which, had it been shorter, could have been one of the genuinely funny parodies of an era. As it stands, it is a gigantic and consequently tiresome spoof of the development of the West, of the traditional heroic Western novel, and of the concept of natural aristocracy that he so laboriously worked out over so many years. In this story of Silver City, Colorado, and of the family of P. J. Meany, who rules an empire of cattle and silver as baronially as he does the family, the town, and the state,

Bromfield magnifies both setting and characters to the point where they are at least four times life-size and twice the size of conventional Westerns. Consequently, the characters are ridiculous in their appetites, their virtues, their villainies, and their searches for fulfillment. P. J.'s determination to buy culture for the community and his subsequent rage at the performers; his violent, futile efforts to subdue his mistress, Madge Beakymer, and the havoc it wreaks on the "cozy corner" of the local brothel; his long cold war with his wife, Ellie-May, who had secretly defeated him years before by having a child by his enemy and who takes refuge in furiously pedalling her new-fangled sewing machine—all these provide a basis of good-natured satire that, had it been less intense, would have been devastating in its impact. As it is, the novel is at its funniest in the sketches of P.J.'s villainous son Blackie, who, when accused of being the orneriest man in town, humbly asserts that he aims to be; in his son Buck's dogged pursuit of the virginal La Belle da Ponte; and in P.J.'s daughter Eudora's self-imposed illness that necessitates her use of a telescope to keep informed on the activities of the town.

If Bromfield had limited himself to such sharp and funny caricatures, the book would have had its desired results; and a surprisingly large number of reviewers, as well as one of the more popular book clubs, would not have taken it to be a seriously presented Western. It is extremely possible, however, that its reception was just what Bromfield intended: that he was not only spoofing the Western, as well as, in Ellie-May and Eudora, both the natural aristocrat and the strong woman, but more importantly the reviewers and readers who had taken him up as his serious reputation went into decline. The people who saw *What Became of Anna Bolton* and *Wild Is the River* as great novels—both of which Bromfield himself regarded as considerably less than mediocre—were the same people who hailed *Colorado* as a great Western novel. Although Bromfield had no real idea of what had gone wrong with these earlier novels because he failed to recognize that neither their characters nor their purpose were important or meaningful to him anymore, nevertheless he must have taken a somber pleasure in the critics' misunderstanding of this. In later years he maintained that *Colorado* was certainly his most misunderstood novel.

Colorado was for Bromfield simply a means of expending sur-

plus creative energy; his main interests remained the farm and
the countryside in spite of the almost constant flow of farmers,
curiosity-seekers, small-town romantics, and celebrities of all
kinds who found their way down Pleasant Valley Road to the
farm, only to be put to work by "the Boss." He remained dedicated to bringing the farm to maximum, self-sustaining production, and he was striving to explain in his writing what he was
attempting to do at the same time that he was trying to understand the hold that the Ohio countryside and the romantic tragedy of its past held on him. Articles continued to appear almost
constantly in magazines ranging from *Reader's Digest* to *The
Atlantic*—each an attempt to do either or both; and *Pleasant
Valley, A Few Brass Tacks,* and *Malabar Farm* were his major
literary efforts. Nevertheless he was to write two more novels,
in each of which he attempted to convey what he felt and what
he had learned. After the last novel he recognized what he
had suspected since he returned to Ohio: that the substance
of his new experiences and beliefs was not the material from
which novels, and certainly not sweeping character-centered
Bromfield novels, could be constructed.

VIII   The Wild Country

In *The Wild Country,* published in 1948, Bromfield made his
only serious attempt to use this material in a novel, although he
must have recognized its futility: Not a bad novel, it is simply
a weak imitation of the depth of feeling in *The Farm* and in his
current nonfiction because he forced himself to concentrate on
the characterization and plot that by this time had become to him
extraneous. Ostensibly set in Missouri, the novel is actually set
in Pleasant Valley and specifically on "Malabar Farm" as it must
have been in the years just prior to World War I, before the
automobile had brought congestion and chaos to the countryside. Consequently the setting shows pastoral peacefulness on
the surface and violent currents of sensuality underneath. In this
novel Bromfield probes both—not merely to define them but to
seek the origin of their mystic unity.

Bromfield's theme in *The Wild Country* is an adaptation of
the traditional romantic view of the loss of childhood innocence
and of the growth of awareness that evil is part of the scheme
of nature. The protagonist is a twelve-year-old boy who lives

with his cultured Jeffersonian grandfather on a Missouri horse farm that is set in the midst of a fertile valley close to a tract of wilderness known as the Wild Country. The boy, Ronnie, first learns of the existence of evil when he overhears a neighbor, Old Virgil, tell his grandfather that Henry, a young neighbor who is Ronnie's hero, has brought home a "chippy" from the World's Fair. The grandfather explains to the boy what a "chippy" is, but he emphasizes, and the boy eventually learns, that the appearance of evil is not necessarily evil itself; in fact, it may merely mask underlying good. The boy accepts this truth as he learns to know and love the girl for her kindness and innate wisdom.

The lessons continue; Ronnie, who has learned to accept matter-of-factly the phenomenon of horse breeding, sees the same viciousness and sheer force manifest themselves in some human beings. Red McGovern, the horse trainer, seduces a half-witted serving girl of Old Virgil who has had designs on the girl himself; his grandfather's protégé Wayne Torrance pursues Henry's new wife; Virgil and his wife Mattie have merely lived in the same house for years; Ronnie's own grandmother had run off with another man years before. Out of this sexual and emotional chaos Ronnie learns, with the aid of his grandfather, to perceive the true difference between good and evil and, most importantly, to probe beneath the surface before accepting the categories imposed by convention upon appearance.

But the novel goes well beyond the theme of adolescent initiation because Bromfield introduces material that gives it a good deal of substance and unfortunately contributes to inherent structural weaknesses. The vivid background of nature, both on the farm and in the Wild Country, is so powerful that at times it emerges as a living thing, unfortunately, to the detriment of the focus upon the interplay of human emotion. The contrast between Henry, who is intrinsically good and clean, and Wayne, the essence of animalistic sexual drive and corruptness, is effectively handled, especially because only the boy suspects that such a dichotomy exists, until the denouement. But the introduction of Vinnie, Henry's wife, to provide a third side to the triangle, results in a sophistication that seems beyond the understanding of an adolescent observer. Bromfield's use of an old Richland County legend to provide a basis for another triangle—that of Virgil, Mattie, and Emma Kleinfelter, the half-witted girl—combines a particularly horrible and yet poetically just double murder with the opportunity for comments on the nature of the world's unsuccessful, weak, and savagely envious have-nots; and in these statements Bromfield foreshadows *Mr. Smith.* At the same time he introduces the material of folklore at the expense of structural and thematic unity. Finally, Ronnie's recognition that his grandmother is a good woman, and his grandfather's acceptance of her after her absence of many years, reinforce the theme but at the expense of credibility.

In spite of these shortcomings, the novel has many strengths. The contrast between the pastoral and peaceful farm and the brutality of the Wild Country effectively emphasizes the nature of human life at the same time that it makes clear the symbolism of the title. The recurring imagery of the physical and the sensual, as well as the sensuous, goes far to explain Ronnie's seemingly mystic identification with nature. The portrayals of the grandfather, who rejects both puritanism and license, and of the grandmother, who is strong enough to do the things her womanly nature demands, are so idealized that they are memorable only because they come close to Bromfield's concept of the Jeffersonian ideal.

Then, too, the novel contains remarkable insights that reveal a maturity in Bromfield's thinking that could have become possible only after his romantic return to the farm. As he points out that the security of Ronnie's youthful world is an illusion and that closeness to nature also implies closeness to all that is base in man, he also indicates the limitations in the world of the valley. It is not the world, even though at times it seems to be a microcosm; and although it is a refuge, it is merely a preliminary doorstep to the infinitely more complex world beyond the hills.

In its probing beyond the rural surface there is much in the novel that is reminiscent of both William Faulkner and Mark Twain, not because Bromfield has turned to them for inspiration but because for the first and only time he is attempting to probe the problems of good and evil to which they devoted the bulk of their attention and because he has used much the same sort of subject matter. In so doing, Bromfield reiterates the nature of their conclusions, and he recognizes, as they have in their works, the complexities of the dichotomy that at once ennobles and degrades man. Although the same sort of pessimism that marks their conclusions permeates the pages of *The Wild Country,* Bromfield refuses to accept its permanence, for the novel ends on a note of optimism impossible to either Faulkner or Mark Twain.

The Wild Country is a radical departure from Bromfield's usual subject matter, theme, and characterization; and the result is neither so bad nor so good as it might have been. As a novel it reveals a great deal of insight into the rural countryside and into the minor tragedies that are absorbed by its permanence. Moreover, this novel is marked by a sensitivity that stands in strong contrast to the shallow sophistication of much of Bromfield's later work. Had it been the product of a novelist at the beginning of a career and not of one about to close a long career, it would have marked the emergence of an important writer.

The Wild Country was followed by a number of articles and by *Out of the Earth,* all of them reflecting Bromfield's continued preoccupation with farming and with other contemporary problems. Nevertheless, it is evident that Bromfield was beginning to lose the intensity of his enthusiasm for "Malabar Farm," probably because almost everything that he set out to do there had been accomplished. The emphasis upon the narrowness of the valley and the wideness of the world beyond it in *The Wild Country* foreshadowed an increasing preoccupation with farm problems elsewhere that was to result in experimental farms in Texas and Brazil and in a more intense preoccupation with social and economic problems. These problems provided the subject matter for his newspaper column "A Voice From the Country" and for much of his nonfiction; they were also the inspiration and the substance for what was to be his last novel, *Mr. Smith.*

IX Mr. Smith

Like *The Wild Country, Mr. Smith,* published in 1951, is quite different from his earlier novels—not, however, because he has explored new themes, characters, or settings, but because, while ostensibly writing a novel, Bromfield has written what is actually a tract. Presented as a long manuscript written by an army captain who is stationed on an isolated South Pacific island in charge of four men guarding supplies, the book alternates between chapters in which the captain analyzes his life at home and chapters in which he attempts to understand the men under his command. The result is a transparent, awkward attempt to portray the five men on the island as representatives of the American dilemma.

Bromfield calls the novel *Mr. Smith* because he sees the captain, Wolcott Ferris—a resident of the best suburb of Oakdale, a typical Midwestern town—as a modern-day Everyman, the basic dilemma of whose life is presumably that of the middle-class man who strives futilely to live a meaningful life. Ferris finds his life at home to be completely devoid of all meaning, and for these reasons: he is dominated by a grasping, superficial, possessive wife whom he has secretly considered murdering; his mother is characterized by the worst features of Philip Wylie's Momism; his two children are rapidly becoming monsters; his business has no need of either intelligence or integrity; and his social group is devoted to noisy, public, purposeless action that fills its emptiness at the same time that it prohibits any sort of meaningful or individual action.

Waiting, suspended in time on the island, Ferris draws these conclusions at the same time that he examines many other facets of modern American life and finds them all to be sterile, ritualized patterns of behavior. Love, education, crowd activity, religion, and the ridiculous symbols such as the "Family of the Year" award given to himself and his family because of the manipulations of his mother, are all totally devoid of honesty, sincerity, or meaning. But these are the symptoms rather than the causes of the American illness that comes from materialism. To Ferris, aloof on his island, it is a disease without hope or cure; American individualism is gone, smothered by a materialistic mass society.

As for the men under his command, Ferris examines each of them as symbolic of a segment of American society. In the sergeant he sees a remnant of the old individualism that had found no place in the mass society; he has taken refuge in an army that provides complete security at the cost of enormous waste in both men and things, and he is destined to wander endlessly, living to satisfy his sensual appetites after the war because there is nothing else for him. Meyer, the Orthodox Brooklyn Jew, is the forever unknown and unknowable; he is introverted and isolated by a tradition as enslaving in its own way as the American materialism that he rejects. Al, the Kansas farm boy, is unimaginative and simple; he is concerned only with his love for the soil and is unaware of the implications of modern society.

In himself and in the last of the enlisted men, Ferris sees in microcosm the social battle raging in the world, of which World War II is only a part. Ferris is the impotent heir of American culture and strength; Homer, the "wool-hat," is symbolic of the future of America and the world. An illiterate, unthinking, coarse, animalistic hillbilly, Homer is one of the have-nots of the world who have found, in the sheer weight of their numbers and consciousless behavior, the strength to assert their demand for a dignity that they do not understand and for rights that they have not earned. One of a new breed of exploiters who takes what he wants and the product of bad environment resulting from a bad heredity that nature cannot redeem, Homer can neither be saved nor prevented from working out his destructive destiny. In the end, Homer, while on guard, accidentally (presumably) shoots Captain Ferris. This act resolves the battle on the island and foretells the outcome of the battle in the world.

Bromfield's pessimism is the product of oversimplification, fear, and, most of all of distrust of any sort of mass action designed either to prevent the sort of crisis that has arisen in the world and on the island or to eliminate the sort of environment that has produced the Homers of the world. Such action is the result of the fuzzy thinking of "do-gooders" whom Bromfield condemns as indulging in wishful thinking that can only aid and abet the have-nots in their drive to dominate and to destroy what they cannot understand. There is nothing that can be done to prevent catastrophe, he asserts; at the end, Ferris is purged and clean but empty; and he and the world that produced him have passed beyond the possibility of salvation.

It is unfortunate that this is the last creative product of a long literary career—not because it admits failure in a search that has driven so many others to despair, but because it is a bad novel. In his effort to reproduce the meandering work of a literary amateur, Bromfield has succeeded too well; the resulting awkwardness in structure and style, the inadequate type characterization, and the oversimplification of interpretation that eliminates all subtleties give the novel the proportions of a diatribe instead of a sympathetic portrayal of a man who is lost and defeated in a world he cannot understand. Upon its appearance, the novel was regarded as a modern *Babbitt*—and Ferris as a new portrayal of the American businessman. But Sinclair Lewis' portrait a generation earlier emphasized Babbitt's humanity; Bromfield asserts that it is too late for such bumbling good intentions. Instead, he has presented in *Mr. Smith* a denial of Babbitt's humanity; and Wolcott Ferris emerges as an inhuman automaton controlled by impotent indignation and despair.

From the farm that has become his island, Bromfield presents an indictment of an entire civilization in *Mr. Smith* at the same time that he admits defeat for the Jeffersonian civilization he sought to reconstruct in his work for so long. As his final fictional statement of the nature of man, as well as the meaning of America, it is a denial of man's dignity, a renunciation of man's hope, and a complete surrender of the principles upon which Bromfield based his life as well as his work. The bitterness that permeates the volume is symptomatic of Bromfield's own despair and frustration; and, most importantly, it provides the key to the decline and fall of a novelist. The answers to man's dilemma that he provided in his early novels were not *the answers*, as the romantic always finds once he has made his escape into what he is convinced is fulfillment; instead, they are the beginning of an even more difficult problem: after escape, then what? In his attempt to answer this question, Bromfield found that there are no answers; after taking refuge in a cynicism that questioned the value of all his work, in *Colorado*, he could either reassert his optimism or go down to despair. *Mr. Smith* is the pathetic result of this personal philosophic dilemma.

CHAPTER 7

A Cubic Foot of Soil

IN THE SEVEN VOLUMES of nonfiction that Bromfield published between 1945 and 1955—the works that eclipsed and finally supplanted his fiction—the image emerges of the complete man as the eighteenth century saw him. These works, ranging from folklore and personal essays through political and economic theory to treatises on practical agriculture, find their inspiration in the dictum of The Enlightenment that through Franklin and Jefferson became part of the mainstream of the American progress that it was designed to foster: the enlightened man must not only apply his reason to his experience and generalize intelligently from the results, but he must publish those results for the inspiration and the information of others. This, Bromfield was determined to do in spite of the outspoken denunciation of the idea by his secretary-critic George Hawkins, to whom such writings were "humus, mucus, retch and vetch," [1] rather than the storytelling that would find a ready market.

It is evident that this major change in the direction, subject matter, and nature of Bromfield's work is neither an accident nor the result of his having written himself out during a literary career in which he published an average of a book a year for more than twenty years. Nor is the change the product of a wishful romanticism that took him back to the valley in Richland County, Ohio, that he knew as a child, although that element enters into the first of the series, *Pleasant Valley*. Rather, the change is the result of the same forces that led him to escape from a town dominated by industry and commerce and for half a lifetime to seek permanence and human values in both his life and his work. Finally, on the other side of the earth from Pleasant Valley, he learned that neither running and regretting nor searching and theorizing were substitutes for the dedication, hard work, and consistent application of intelligence to the natural order that is the only way man can find a measure of fulfillment and meaning in a chaotic world. The name "Malabar" that he selected for the farm signifies what he learned in India at the same time that it pays tribute to a piece of beautiful land.

I Pleasant Valley

Pleasant Valley, the first book-length product of Bromfield's return to Ohio, appeared in the spring of 1945. In it Bromfield tells the story of his return and of the first six years of the farming venture. As he re-creates his deep sense of identification with both the Ohio past and the countryside, he reveals, too, the nature of the romantic dream of Jeffersonian and Rousseauan self-sufficiency that led him back; the equally romantic dream that inspired him to attempt the restoration of land which had been abandoned by men far more experienced than he in practical agriculture and economics; and the sometimes grim but always instructive reality that modified the first of these dreams while it gave life, in a very real sense, to the second.

In *Pleasant Valley* Bromfield finds no need for the pseudo-sophistication or the superficiality that marred much of his last fiction; instead, because he had at last found a way of life that was meaningful and demanding, as well as a subject matter that was infinitely complex beneath its seemingly simple surface, he found that he could write directly, forcefully, and honestly of the things that to him were at the heart of any possible meaning in life. In a series of loosely connected essays he describes his rediscovery of the valley, the stories behind the farms and houses that were brought together as "Malabar Farm," the building of the "Big House," and the agricultural theory and practice that resulted in the rejuvenation of soil that had been ruthlessly mined for a century.

The most revealing section of the book describes the plan under which "Malabar Farm" was to be operated. As conceived, it was an agricultural, economic, and social experiment that combined capitalistic free enterprise with social planning and mild collectivism—a scheme not entirely unlike that of some of the early New Deal "braintrusters" whom Bromfield had begun to castigate publicly during the presidential campaign of 1940. The goals of the farming operation were the complete restoration to full production of the eroded hillside farms and the economic security of the families who worked them. To accomplish these goals, Bromfield envisioned combining sound agricultural practices that would restore organic and mineral matter to the soil—largely through the use of trash and grass farming—with the raising of crops that would result in production of everything needed for subsistence on the farm itself except coffee, spices, and sugar. In effect his goal was the re-creation of a way of life that had vanished in America as soil washed down to the sea and as abstract forces of economics gained their ascendency during the years of exploitation that had begun in the Civil War era and had turned America away from the Jeffersonian dream of an agricultural democracy. As such, Bromfield's dream was the culmination of a long romantic search; but it was a dream that, as *Pleasant Valley* and the other agricultural works candidly admit, had to be modified many times as the facts of economic life in twentieth-century America made themselves felt.

But the book is a great deal more than the record of Bromfield's return to the land and his dream of agricultural and pastoral fulfillment. The best essays in the book, some of which are among Bromfield's most effective and most deeply felt work, are those that deal with the countryside itself and with the people, the animals, and the legends that give it life. In "Up Ferguson Way" he combines the beauty and wildness of the countryside with the tragic aura that hangs mystically over it in the spirits of dead and degenerate Indians, in the stones that mark the sites of vanished cabins, and in the relentlessness with which nature eradicates the footprints of man. In "Johnny Appleseed and Aunt Mattie" he re-creates the legends of the mystic, half-wild John Chapman, who provides the basis of much Midwestern legend, and of the equally mysterious and tragic Eleazer Williams, who, half-mad, found widespread acceptance as the Lost Dauphin. But Bromfield does not merely retell their stories; instead he makes these characters live in the cycle of birth, growth, death, decay, and rebirth that characterizes the essentially unchanged life in the valley as he had discovered it as a boy and had found it on his return in middle age.

In these sections he sets forth the premise that dominates the sections in which he retells valley legends such as "On Being 'Teched,'" "My Ninety Acres," and the story of the half-witted girl who poisoned her family. At the same time he reiterates the philosophy that provides the basis for his farming and his social experiments. A concept as common in the eighteenth century as it is rare in the twentieth, it is the premise that God and Nature have produced an orderly universe governed by immutable laws, the most obvious of which is the life cycle, and that man violates them only at his peril. Conversely, by discovering those laws, by emulating them in his own life, and by working with them rather than against them in the world of nature, man comes closest to understanding the ultimate nature of the universe at the same time that he approaches understanding of himself.

In discovering and working in harmony with these laws through the application of reason to experience, Bromfield depends on an approach that is more romantic than rational, however. The quality of being "teched"—that is capable of experiencing a mystic kinship with and understanding of nature and of animals to the extent that intuition and empathy transcend physical and biological barriers—is, Bromfield maintains, essential to understanding nature and to using it by serving it through the laws that cannot be learned except through experience and desire.

As a whole, *Pleasant Valley* is Bromfield's *Walden;* and the relationship between the two books is obvious. Not only is Bromfield's attempt to define the complete life of the complete man very close to Thoreau's, but the two books are very close in structure, in theme, and in purpose. In *Pleasant Valley* Bromfield uses the particulars of his return, his experiences, and his observations on the farm as points of departure for examining the universal significances of man's relationship to nature and to nature's God, as did Thoreau's predecessors in the eighteenth century. But then, like Thoreau, Bromfield returns from those universals to the particulars of one man's individual experiences, making *Pleasant Valley,* like *Walden,* the microcosm of man's experience as he attempts to find his place in the natural order through reason, observation, empathy, intuition, and whatever other techniques bring him closer to that discovery. Thoreau carried through his self-identification on the shores of Walden Pond and, in the process, discovered the rules of nature that were to dominate the rest of his life; for Bromfield the discovery came along the banks of Switzer's Creek and in the field and woods of "Malabar Farm."

In summary, *Pleasant Valley* provides the basis for Bromfield's personal, agricultural, and economic philosophies as they were made clear in his nonfiction of the 1940's and 1950's and as they were followed in the agricultural practices on "Malabar Farm." He believed that by following these principles one might find fulfillment in his own life, richness in agriculture, and peace in the economic, social, and political worlds. In the final analysis, the secrets of life, he believed, are contained in a cubic foot of top soil. If one discovers them by whatever means are necessary, even through the intuition of being "teched," he can then construct the perfect world.

II   A Few Brass Tacks

Bromfield followed *Pleasant Valley* with *A Few Brass Tacks* (1946). He asserts in the "Apologia" with which he prefaces this book that it does not provide the answers to man's problems in the world, the nation, or even his own township; but in it he attempts to carry on what he had begun in *Pleasant Valley* by seeking to discover the causes of imbalance that threaten to destroy the world. His era is an "Age of Irritation," he declares, in which man's genius has been perverted by materialism and has been turned into destructive rather than constructive channels; the result is a constant irritation that threatens to produce a cancer fatal to civilization.

The basic problem that produces this irritation, he maintains, is the belief that all man's problems are material and that they can be solved by material means. This belief implies that they can be solved by money or by the manipulation of money. The entire course of the modern world, he asserts, has been determined by this easy but false answer; and it is hurrying man to destruction. Bromfield does not imply, however, that he understands the complexity of modern economic chaos or that he can provide solutions. He is, he says, attempting to clarify his own thinking and, if possible, to stimulate the thinking of others—even at the expense of abuse.

The result did stimulate a great deal of abuse for two reasons: first, because the result in many respects is much like a freshman course in pre-Keynesian conservative economics; and second because it marks the beginning of Bromfield's continued attacks on New and Fair Deal economics. In the book Bromfield accepts and approves, however, of much social and economic legislation, sponsored by both, particularly that relative to business control and to labor relations. It marks too the beginning of his close alliance with political forces of the economic right, as represented by Frank Lausche and Robert Taft.

Nevertheless, in his attempts to distinguish causes from effects and to reassert spiritual values that have been lost or ignored in the onslaught of materialism that has engulfed the world since the triumph of the industrial revolution, Bromfield comes close to some fundamental truths; but his interpretations of their significances are often distorted or mistaken. Industrialization, he maintains, has intensified the confusion between money and wealth, an ancient delusion that dominates America's thinking today; and of course he is right. The cult of the businessman, with its deification of ledgers, balanced budgets, profits, and black ink, has hidden the truth that money is merely an inadequate and often inaccurate means for measuring the true wealth that lies in a country's human and natural resources. Yet much of the tragedy of modern life, from depressions and runaway inflations that paralyze the world down to individual domestic tragedies, is the result of that confusion of a means with an end. This is a truism that has been repeated and ignored, as Bromfield recognizes, for many years; yet he points out that the distinction must be made and accepted, in spite of the advertising myth-making that contributes to the confusion. In this assertion he reiterates, with more vigor and less faith, the portrayal of *Puzzled America* that Sherwood Anderson provided in his vivid and human reporting of the Depression. But whereas Bromfield writes of the results of confusion in abstractions that grow out of love for the soil, Anderson writes in terms of realities that grow out of a love for and faith in individual human beings.

In the chapter on "Agriculture in Relation to our National Economy" Bromfield asserts that the basis of the American economy and social structure lies in our farms; and it is in this area that modern economists and politicians have made their most serious mistakes. Completely rejecting the economic pragmatism of the New and Fair Deals, he asserts that controls, regulations, and subsidies merely intensify the problem by encouraging the exploitation of our soil through the inefficient and wasteful practices that send so much of it into the sea. This problem is moot; it has provided fuel for debates that are likely to continue as long as farming is regarded as a sacred way of life by so many—both by those who support and by those who oppose governmental controls. However, it is hard to quarrel with Bromfield's assertion that an agricultural surplus is a mirage in a hungry world, that the problem lies in faulty distribution rather than artificial control. But to this problem he has no solution.

Bromfield reinforces the premises made in the first two chapters of *A Few Brass Tacks* in "Thomas Jefferson versus Karl Marx." In this chapter he employs the contrasts inherent in the economic philosophies of the two men to demonstrate the validity of his and Jefferson's belief that only agriculture can provide a solid and real economic base for the country; Marx's position, he maintains, is the result of the confusion between money and real wealth. In this chapter, however, there are many paradoxes in Bromfield's position; and these paradoxes isolate him from twentieth-century American conservatism at the same time that they draw him philosophically closer to the New and Fair Deal policies that he so frequently attacks. Effectively, if unconsciously, he links the democracy of Jefferson with that of Roosevelt and Truman.

Although he believes with Jefferson that great cities are intrinsically evil and dehumanizing and that racial and economic oppressions will disappear only when man returns to a life close to nature, he accepts the social reforms that have led to better housing, fair employment practices, and the other liberal acts of legislation of the 1930's, reserving his highest praise for the work of the Tennessee Valley Authority, the perennial target of the political Right. Bromfield describes this masterpiece of social planning as the perfect example of democracy in action as well as an ideal pattern for what must be done in each of America's great watersheds.

An even more radical departure from the Right lies in his interpretation of the meaning of imperialistic communism. This system, he maintains, is not the source of the world's ills as so many on the Right maintain; it is merely a result of the confusion that believes these ailments can be cured by materialistic rather than by spiritual means. Man, he believes, is a spiritual animal; and he can save himself only by a return to the humanistic principles of Jefferson—not by the materialistic premises of capitalism or communism which promise to save him today.

A *Few Brass Tacks* is perhaps as close to a complete expression of Jeffersonianism as is possible in the world today. Although much of it sounds naïve, and certainly some of it is outdated, Bromfield nevertheless recognizes and denounces the effects of industrialism as effectively and as perceptively as his great predecessor. More importantly, however, it makes clear that Bromfield was not the reactionary that he has been so frequently called; and it indicates that his political alliance with the American Right was primarily one of convenience, based on his opposition to governmental acts that he saw as wasteful or doomed. The social legislation that promised to solve basic problems he accepted wholeheartedly, just as he praised the relationship between the TVA and the farmers of the Tennessee Valley; but the broad pattern of symptom-treating in acreage controls, subsidies, and stop-gap measures, he denounced as ill-considered, naïve, and destructive. In spite of its tendency toward oversimplification (perhaps necessary in view of the popular audience he was aiming to reach), repetition, and awkwardness that is unusual in Bromfield's normally vigorous prose, and political biases that are often intolerant as well as lacking in perception, A *Few Brass Tacks* is an eloquent Jeffersonian document.

III Malabar Farm

By 1948, in spite of wartime difficulties, Bromfield had to a great extent completed many of the projects for the farm that he had 'outlined in *Pleasant Valley*. In a fashion *Malabar Farm*, published in the spring of 1948, is a sequel to that volume because it records the successes and failures of the vast experimental program he carried out. Prefaced and concluded by letters to an army sergeant who had presumably written Bromfield for information about agriculture as a possible postwar occupation, the volume is partially an elementary textbook on the farming practices employed at "Malabar." But the technical chapters are interspersed with sections from Bromfield's journal and from several personal essays which are much like those that give *Pleasant Valley* its air of universality.

In spite of its looseness and its variety in form, the book is unified by the introductory and concluding letters, by its subject matter, its eminently readable style, and its organization, which depicts the cycle of growth and decay that takes place during a year on the farm. The core of the book is the minute description of agricultural trials, errors, and successes that take place during the year; the journal sections add both immediacy and personality; and essays such as those on the farm pond and the flood of 1947 provide implications of the universal significances behind the experiments at "Malabar."

This combination of forms and subjects gives insight into Bromfield's purpose and his accomplishment in the volume. Bromfield was certainly writing for the practical farmer as well as for those who, like the army sergeant, were sentimentally looking into the possibilities of an agricultural career. But more importantly, he was writing to a general, literate audience about the practical application of the theories he had inherited from The Enlightenment and about their practical results as well as theoretical implications. In *Malabar Farm* he begins by assuming as self-evident that nature has achieved a perfect balance in the continuous cycle of birth, growth, reproduction, death, decay, and rebirth that governs the natural order. Thus, in typical eighteenth-century fashion, he asserts that man must emulate that order in agricultural practice if he is to be successful and at the same time to restore the earth. But first he must discover that order through applying his reason to the experience derived from observation and experimentation and from carefully examining and evaluating the results. Like Franklin's *Autobiography*, *Malabar Farm* is, then, Bromfield's effort to make the record of those observations, experiments, and conclusions available for the information, edification, and contemplation of those who, like himself, are attempting to make order out of chaos.

The resulting volume is much more than an introduction to Bromfield's theory of natural farming. Its often painful honesty, its deep empathy with living things, and its consistent efforts to explain and interpret make it what it is: the search for an elusive but nevertheless attainable order in an aspect of life that has largely been lost in the twentieth century. In *Malabar Farm*, suddenly, like the springs that had long before dried up as a result of man's abuses, that aspect of life is alive and meaningful again. In describing the renewal of ruined soil, Bromfield is also depicting the renewal of human life that has been ruined by the impersonal and dehumanizing practices of a century dominated by greed. Just as grass, time, and organic matter give life and substance to a depleted and inert soil, so man's dedication, determination, and a reverence for and understanding of nature give meaning and life to him.

The most revealing sections of the book in this respect are "The Cycle of a Farm Pond" and "Some More Animals." They clearly illustrate the close relationship between man and nature that Bromfield asserts is necessary if man is to find meaning and purpose in his life, and they are worthy of inclusion in any anthology of the best nature writing of our time. In "The Cycle" he presents in microcosm the achievement of balance in the natural order, the observation and emulation of that balance in detail, and the implications that it holds for the macrocosm of the pond that is man's world. In "Some More Animals" he exemplifies the intuitive aspects of being "teched" as they lead man to a closer understanding of his environment.

But as a whole, the book exhibits much of the hasty preparation and writing that marred too much of Bromfield's work. The repetitious elements in the book could have been eliminated easily and mechanically; transitions and unity in style would have contributed much to a unity of structure that would have given support to his unified thesis. These shortcomings will prevent *Malabar Farm* from achieving first rank among volumes of nature writing, but they do not obscure the basic worth of the book as a valuable contribution to a problem that is vital to the continued existence and well-being of man in a world that is every day more crowded and less productive. *Malabar Farm* is the testimony of Bromfield's faith that these problems can be solved if man wants to solve them badly enough and if he looks to nature for their solutions. The validity of his conclusions may be questioned, as they have been by agricultural experts; but the honesty of the book and the evidence of the green hills and flowing springs of "Malabar" provide testimony that weighs heavily in Bromfield's favor. However, evaluation and final judgment of this work is beyond the province of literary criticism.

The most significant biographical detail in *Malabar Farm* is not what Bromfield accomplished, but his recognition, as a result of experience and the realities of economics, that the most romantic part of his dream could not become fact. Instead of the self-sustaining farm that would produce a rich, full life through diversified agriculture, "Malabar Farm" actually became a specialized venture, as Bromfield ruefully acknowledges, a factory in which grass was turned into the meat and bone of marketable animals. But the garden on which he lavished a great deal of care flourished as if denying that fact, and his point of pride that the "Malabar" achievement could be duplicated anywhere by any farmer of limited means was for him adequate compensation.

By 1950 "Malabar Farm" was nearing its maximum productive capacity, and Bromfield, recognizing that it was making fewer and less intense demands on both his imagination and his time, began to seek other outlets for his energy and opportunities to put his theories and his experiences to practical use elsewhere. "Malabar Farm," for which he had not lost his enthusiasm, had become a focal point for farmers, agricultural scientists, and the curious public from all parts of the world. Their interest and questions led him to do two things: to describe the "Malabar" experience as completely as he could in order to answer all the questions about it, and to begin to put his practical experience to work and to test his theories under other soil and climatic conditions. The latter led to his agreement to serve in an advisory capacity in the establishment of "Malabar Farm" in Texas near Wichita Falls; founded by a group of Texans, it was an experiment in semi-arid agriculture. Later Bromfield served in the same capacity for a similar project, "Malabar-do-Brasil," in South America. Although he found some tranquility on his trips to Brazil, he found peace increasingly difficult to attain in Ohio, as his personal life began to disintegrate with the deaths of his parents, especially his mother; of George Hawkins; and of his wife, Mary. These losses were followed within a few years by the marriages of his daughters Hope and Ellen.

IV   Out of the Earth

Bromfield's decision to answer all of the questions about the agricultural practices at "Malabar" led to *Out of the Earth,* published in the spring of 1950. In many ways this volume was the agricultural textbook that its predecessors were not; in others it is further evidence that not even the most pedestrian subject matter could eliminate either the intensity of his enthusiasm or the power over words which enabled him to probe beyond the immediate and to approach the universals. As a whole, however, the exposition of agricultural practices predominate. Consequently, the book is better organized than *Malabar Farm* and its reception was almost entirely in agricultural terms.

Bromfield's thesis in *Out of the Earth* is the same which dominates his other agricultural works: that depleted soils can be renewed through restoration of a natural balance by practices that can be followed by any farmer anywhere who takes into consideration the variables of subsoil, climate, and rainfall. In developing this thesis, his purpose is to disseminate widely in nontechnical language the results of the "Malabar" experiment which, he maintained, was actually not radical innovation but merely the application of the best agricultural thinking. Thus the book goes well beyond the confines of "Malabar Farm"; it is a serious effort to bring together and make available the theory and experimental results of what he designated as the greatest advances in agricultural practice in man's history. The result is Bromfield's major agricultural work.

In it he traces briefly the close relationship that still exists between the balance of nature in the sea, out of which all living things come, and man's environment; he discusses the theories that provide the basis for restoring that balance in the soil and the theories that relate the soil to man's health and well-being; he discusses the possible control of insect pests and of animal disease through natural means; and, most importantly in an age in which water shortages and floods are increasingly serious problems, the restoration of balance in that area also. In occasional digressions, he explores the relationship of elements as diverse as wild life, regional problems, and the structure of farm machinery to progressive agricultural practices. And finally, foreshadowing *A New Pattern for a Tired World,* his sequel to *A Few Brass Tacks,* he asserts that the world can feed itself if it is willing to dedicate itself to the practices that will make such self-sufficiency possible.

The epilogue, "A Philosophical Excursion," is Bromfield's effort to move all of the practical discussion into the realm of absolute meaning by exploring its ramifications in terms of the significance of man's life. While it does not reach those heights because Bromfield finds his fulfillment in a sensuous rather than a spiritual awareness of the meaning of the good life, it is an eloquent statement, nevertheless, of the faith behind the "Malabar" experiment and of the sense of permanence and fulfillment that he has found in carrying it out. From the total experience he has learned much:

> But most of all there is the earth and the animals through which one comes very close to eternity and to the secrets of the universe. Out of Gus, the Mallard duck, who comes up from the pond every evening to eat with the dogs, out of Stinker, the bull, with his wise eyes and placid disposition, out of all the dogs which run ahead leaping and barking and luring the small boys farther and farther into the fields, a child learns much, and most of all that warmth and love of Nature which is perhaps the greatest of all resources, not only because its variety and beauty is inexhaustible but because slowly it creates a sense of balance and values, of philosophy and even of wise resignation to man's own insignificance which bring the great rewards of wisdom and understanding and tolerance.[2]

Here—at the time in Bromfield's life in which he feels he has come closest to discovering the ultimate secrets of meaning and satisfaction, and at the beginning of the final phase of his life, in which he was to lose much of his enthusiasm and take refuge in a stubborn, isolated individualism rather than proclaim his faith proudly—is the basis of the philosophy that had dominated both his life and his work for thirty years. It is as close to a definitive statement as he was to make.

Out of the Earth was controversial, as indeed Bromfield intended it to be. Its partisans and opponents made it the most widely discussed and evaluated agricultural book of the epoch. Much of the criticism came from professional experts who were annoyed at the intrusion of a layman into their province and, perhaps more significantly, because he was so certain he was right. But Bromfield took special pride in the fact that his files at "Malabar" began to bulge with letters from practical farmers and people who were genuinely interested in improved agricultural practices, all of whom found stimulation, instruction, and a sense of dedicated direction in the book.

V A New Pattern for a Tired World

In 1954 Bromfield published his most ambitious socio-economic work, the basis of which was a plan that had been germinating and developing in his mind since the end of World War II and had been spurred on to completion by Communist expansion and threats since 1948. Definitively titled *A New Pattern for a Tired World,* it appeared at a time when a great many people were seeking a panacea; and Bromfield, while aware that the problems were too complex for an easy solution, used the book to examine the world situation in terms of his experience and to advance some suggested approaches to solutions rather than to solve them as the title suggests.

In his new pattern for a world exhausted by two major wars and a series of lesser ones in a century little more than half over; threatened by competing economic, political, and social philosophies; and inundated by the outpouring of words designed to sell everything from gadgets to ideas to a gullible public, Bromfield asserts that man can look only to the natural balance of the world for a model upon which to reconstruct his ailing and aged society. Essentially, he sees the source of economic, social, and political evil in the world to be a society which has ignored that balance, which has accepted the premise that all troubles can be cured by financial manipulation, and which has placed its faith in the promise of a materialistic heaven on earth. The result has been a century of revolution engendered by these manipulations and dreams.

The answer, he says, lies in an economic revolution, but not one that, like communism, merely promises to redistribute wealth, or, like western materialism, places its faith in an augmented purchasing power. Instead, the economic revolution, led by the United States, must reconstruct the world in terms of economic units, each unit containing a perfect balance of varied agriculture, resources, geography, industry, consumption, and population. He sees four such units as necessary; the Western Hemisphere; Russia, China, and Japan; India, Pakistan, and peripheral areas; and Western Europe. He asserts that each of these units would be balanced within itself, each would be firmly committed to conservative progress by the existence of a strong middle class, and each would be a self-sustaining part of a perfectly balanced world.

This gradually established balance, begun with a determined and positive approach to solving the economic problems of the Western Hemisphere and then extended to the other areas, attacking each as a unit, would, he maintains, be a logical and positive attempt to solve problems that have thus far been approached in a piecemeal, shotgun fashion. Such an attempt would make unnecessary the patchwork of foreign aid for various purposes, the many agencies of the United Nations, foreign policies that merely regard communism as the evil and vainly strive to contain it, and material production that leads to the aimlessness of a spiritual vacuum.

Essentially Bromfield's plan is that which he employed on "Malabar Farm," but it is greatly magnified to encompass the entire world. On the farm his plan had regarded each area as a unit to be developed in accordance with its natural potential, and then each unit was to be integrated into the whole. It had proven successful in the hills of Richland County, Ohio, on the farm that he had come to see as the microcosm of the world; and he could see no reason why the plan might not be successful when applied to the macrocosm. Recognizing the immensity as well as the complexity of what he suggests, nevertheless he maintains that faith, determination, and wisdom—using the world of nature as a pattern and, by implication, "Malabar" as a model— would make it a success. The world, like the farm, would become a place of peace, richness, and security rather than of fear and evil.

It is easy to quarrel with the plan on the basis of its scope, its arbitrary nature, and its failure to take into consideration the national, regional, local, and human factors that conspire against any such effort. And it is difficult to assent to the vast amount of objective and often dehumanized planning that Bromfield, the avowed enemy of a dehumanized world, implies would be necessary if the plan were to be attempted. Most of all, it is difficult, in the twentieth century, to accept the panacea-like premise inherent in the plan, just as it is impossible to find any measure of acceptance for the specific evidence, capable of innumerable interpretations, that he marshals to reject the present attempts to reorder the world and to support the logicality of his approach. But it is impossible to question the conviction with which Bromfield approaches problems as serious and demanding as these and asserts that they can be solved.

A good many portions of *A New Pattern for a Tired World* can be pointed to as indicative of Bromfield's deep economic and political conservatism. In his attacks upon New Deal and Fair Deal policies, and especially upon the foreign policy of

Harry Truman and Dean Acheson, he is often unmerciful—just as he was in his newspaper column of the same time; and the attacks sound much like the campaign speeches of Senator Robert Taft. But there is one important difference. Whereas political conservatism attacked those policies because they were seen as too radical, too advanced, and too dominated by an increasingly powerful government, Bromfield attacks them because they are not radical enough. He maintains that they are too tightly tied to the outmoded and unworkable policies of the past rather than dedicated to future progress through careful planning and execution of what he asserts is a rational, realistic plan. In his proposal, in his international outlook, and in his denunciations of narrow nationalistic self-interest and of the military faction that perpetuates its position by merchandising fear, Bromfield is quite radical, certainly radical enough to cause sleepless nights for the extreme Right, as well as for the Left which had already identified him as a threat.

In the volume Bromfield's radicalism is as evident as that of his social and economic mentor, Thomas Jefferson. Just as Jefferson saw in the eighteenth century that political revolution was meaningless and futile unless it was accompanied by a profound and sweeping social revolution, so Bromfield points out that the same thing is necessary in the twentieth century. At the core of Jefferson's proposal was a firm belief in both the goodness and the wisdom of man; he believed that, given his freedom and the proper direction, man would progress to an ultimate but attainable perfection. In Bromfield's plan—in spite of its weaknesses, its oversimplifications, and its ignorance of the social and economic forces that he professes to understand—a clear echo of the same faith that motivated Jefferson can be heard.

When it was published, *A New Pattern for a Tired World* engendered much the same sort of controversy that Bromfield was accustomed to, as it still does; and perhaps that was Bromfield's major purpose. As it stands, it is both a logical culmination to a philosophy that he had been formulating for the previous twenty years and a sequel to the attacks on an unsatisfactory political and economic structure that he had begun in *England, A Dying Oligarchy* and carried on in *A Few Brass Tacks*. But it was to be his last major attempt to examine the problems of a complex and confused world. Bromfield himself was tired; in spite of his interest in the farm and in the projects in Texas and Brazil, he began to think in terms of an autobiography that would attempt to define the meaning of his experience as he had lived it. The result of this preliminary thinking was his last full-length book, a memoir of himself as he began, for the second time in his life, to look backward instead of ahead in order to find the ultimate fulfillment that he had been seeking.

VI   From My Experience

This book, published in the fall of 1955, is *From My Experience*, a glimpse into the life of a lonely man who has known a great deal of satisfaction and who is reasonably certain that his life has been worth-while in spite of the occasional doubts that foreshadow a decline into old age. Nevertheless, it is a recounting of what he feels was the major decision in his life, the decision to return to Ohio; a recollection of the experiences that justified it and gave his life both meaning and direction; and finally a statement of what he believes the meaning of man's life to be.

The bulk of the volume contains little that is new, and much of that is technical rather than literary; Bromfield even goes so far as to include a formal report on the feasibility of the establishment of "Malabar-do-Brasil" as well as a projected agricultural program for it. Moreover, the material in chapters such as "It Can't be Done," "A Somewhat Technical Chapter," "Our Agricultural Economic Dilemma," and "On Building Topsoils" are repetitious of the earlier agricultural volumes. These chapters were obviously included to give form to what would otherwise have been a thin volume more personal than Bromfield was willing for it to be. But interspersed among these chapters are those that give much insight into Bromfield's appraisal of his life; they are some of the most personal essays that he was to write.

The first chapter, "After Fifteen Years," provides the basis for that reappraisal. He admits candidly that he was attempting to escape the reality of a world gone mad by retreating into the romantic past. He was sick of the world itself and of his own craft as a writer of fiction, a craft that had promised fulfillment but had merely given him fame and fortune. But in seeking the security of the past he found what so many other romantics have found under the same circumstances. For Bromfield the discovery was harsh and real; when the snow melted from Pleasant Valley, he found how badly it had been ravaged by time and men. Thus, he was forced abruptly into a realistic readjustment of his romantic dream to a practical plan that brought hard work, disappointments, pleasure, and a sense of fulfillment he had never known before.

The last chapter, "The White Room," describes his final realization of what he had been attempting to do at "Malabar" and in the years since he had returned to Ohio. In the peace of the room set aside for his use at "Malabar-do-Brasil," he encountered in Albert Schweitzer's *Out of My Life and Thought* the phrase "reverence for life." This, he suddenly realized, was what had dominated his life from the beginning and had sent him back to the farm; this principle, he realized, was what had given his life meaning. In seeking to understand nature and to work with it instead of against it, he had been unconsciously following the principle that Schweitzer expressed so succinctly in a phrase. This principle, put into practice at "Malabar," gave his life the meaning he had been seeking; not only was it all there was in his life, but it was all that he had ever needed or wanted. In the process, Bromfield had become, as he suddenly realized, the complete man, able to identify the elements that make up the meaningful life and to make them his own.

Among other chapters, part of "A Hymn to Hawgs" and "The Hard-working Spring and the House Nobody Loved," are part of his best nature writing and mythmaking. But the substance of the book lies in the first and last chapters, for these are the nearest to pure autobiography. Although there is some evidence to indicate that he was thinking of using them as the basis for a full autobiography, it was never started. Perhaps he realized that, in these two essays and in thirty books written over a period of more than thirty years, he had said it all at one time or another in one or more of the many forms he had used.

VII Animals and Other People

After *From My Experience* was published, Bromfield had little more than a year to live; but during that year he brought out one more book, *Animals and Other People*. In this book, largely made up of the best of the essays that appeared in the books

from *Pleasant Valley* to *From My Experience,* Bromfield illustrates most clearly what Schweitzer's phrase meant to him.
Essentially the collection is about "wild and domestic animals
and about people who are 'teched' and have that inner sense of
mystical feeling which makes them one with Nature and with
animals and birds"; [3] it is, as Bromfield learned the term, a book
about the reverence for life, a reverence that is especially important because, as he comments in the introductory note, in terms
reminiscent of Mark Twain as well as Albert Schweitzer:

> In the last analysis we are all animals and the fact of being
> born a man does not endow us with any special rights or virtues;
> rather it imposes upon us obligations of a high sort indeed,
> which animals and birds do not share—obligations of intelligence,
> ethics, decency, loyalty and moral behavior. The sad thing is how
> frequently these obligations are violated and ignored by man
> himself. [4]

Among the essays are those in which the family pets—dogs,
cats, and even a mongoose—become believable idiosyncratic individuals, as do Sylvester the bull and the hogs whom he had
learned to appreciate. But more important in the collection is
the evidence, gathered together for the first time, of what it
meant to Bromfield to regard himself as "teched," to be able to
understand intuitively the workings of nature, as do old Phoebe
Wise, Walter Oakes of the remarkable ninety-acre farm, and
Aunt Mattie, who in reliving the legend of Johnny Appleseed
became part of that legend herself. More importantly, the inclusion of "The Cycle of a Farm Pond" shows how thoroughly
Bromfield himself was one of that limited group who somehow
"understood," just as so many years before, long before he
returned to "Malabar," he had tried to show Miss Annie Spragg's
mystic understanding.

Animals and Other People is pleasant if repetitious. The collection as a whole indicates the success Bromfield might have
had as a nature writer, and it is more evidence to support the
obvious fact that Bromfield had found a measure of satisfaction,
understanding, and peace at "Malabar" that he had been unable
to find in a career of frenzied writing. As the last book of a
long career, it is important, too, because it is his final acknowledgment of what he found to be life's meaning, a meaning that
takes on profundity through its simplicity.

There is no evidence that Bromfield planned to write anything new or of a more substantial nature after *Animals and Other People;* certainly it seemed that after *Mr. Smith* he was forever done with fiction, a literary form that, he had begun to assert, was futile when it was not fraudulent. His farming material, with the exception of specialized accounts of experiments at "Malabar-do-Brasil," was largely exhausted. Perhaps he might have sought a new direction and a new interest, but during much of 1955 he was ailing; in February, 1956, he returned to "Malabar" from New York after a rest at Doris Duke's farm. Just after he returned he collapsed, and on March 18, 1956, he died at University Hospital in Columbus, Ohio.

At his death he was surrounded and overwhelmed by ironies that perhaps he had foreseen but refused to acknowledge. His last official act in the management of "Malabar Farm" was a testimonial to his individualism at the same time that it was a breach of his determination to preserve the natural balance of the soil: he sold watershed timber from hilltop trees in order to raise money to pay his hospital bill. Following his death, economic forces conspired to prevent the continuance of a family center, and his daughters were compelled to sell the farm. Fortunately, however, as The Louis Bromfield Ecological Center, operated by a foundation, it carries on in his spirit and memory.

CHAPTER *8*

Louis Bromfield in Retrospect

AT BROMFIELD'S DEATH it was widely believed that there had been two Louis Bromfields: the promising young novelist who had gone on to commercial success in a flamboyantly fashionable world before disappearing, and the conservative middle-aged farmer whose dirt-stained fingers wrote convincingly of agricultural practices and alarmingly about economics. This view has largely persisted among his major audiences, the literary groups of the 1920's, the readers of popular fiction in the 1930's, and the agricultural theorists and practitioners of the 1940's and 1950's. To each group, his death was a surprise for a different reason.

At the time of his death his literary reputation was as varied as his audiences. Among recognized literary critics, he was not taken seriously in spite of kind comments by some reviewers about his last fiction. With the reading audiences of the book clubs and the public libraries, interested in fast-moving stories rather than in form and ideas, he remained extremely popular; and with the readers of his agricultural works he was controversially regarded as almost anything from a charlatan to a prophet. In spite of this diversity of audience and opinion based on the apparent dichotomy in his writing career, it is obvious that no such dichotomy exists. Bromfield's lifelong writings were actually the record of a consistent romantic search, and the apparent breaks in his career were merely tactical movements that he hoped would bring him closer to its end.

This unity behind his apparently different careers is evident from the consistency with which he sought to define and to attain a Jeffersonian ideal that had apparently become an anachronism in a society dominated by industrial materialism. His first tactical movement—the departure from Mansfield when it became impossible to revive the family farm as World War I marked the triumph of materialism—was his first attempt to define and attain the Jeffersonian dream. He left Mansfield because he had temporarily acceded to his mother's belief that the natural aristocrat was duty-bound to rise both by rejecting the material standards of the pseudo-aristocracy and by attaining success in artistic and humanistic activities. At the same time this first movement marked the temporary decline of his father's dream of a life of free agrarian dignity and plenty in a natural environment. This decision implied his belief that his father's dream had become impossible in the modern world; and, at the same time, it provided the theme of his panel novels—all of which are attempts to define the nature of the defeat of the agrarian Jeffersonian dream and to proclaim the ultimate triumph of the natural aristocrat over materialism.

However, writing these first novels taught him that the triumph of the natural aristocrat was appearance only because it was essentially a victory based upon the terms of materialism and because, in gaining it, his natural aristocrats had lost the touch with humanity and nature that is essential for fulfillment. But this realization came slowly, intensifying in each of the novels, until in *A Good Woman* his protagonist suffers obvious defeat rather than apparent victory. In *The Green Bay Tree* Lily Shane had apparently escaped the dehumanizing influence of the town, but at the end she has nothing with which to fill her life except melancholy waiting; in *Possession* Ellen Tolliver is completely dehumanized by the goal she has attained, and she is as dominated and isolated by her music as the people of the town are by materialism. In *Early Autumn* there is no victory but a graceful defeat as Olivia Pentland finds herself trapped by dead tradition. *A Good Woman* marks the ultimate defeat as Philip Downes seeks his fulfillment in death after having recognized the transience and the meaninglessness of a victory gained at the expense of human values.

When he recognized the futility of the attempt to escape through adapting the premise of natural aristocracy to a modern, post-Darwinian world, Bromfield had no choice but to abandon the attempt and the rest of the series of projected panel novels. Attempts to escape the modern world through success in the arts could only mean a success on the world's own meaningless material terms. In seeking to provide a meaningful victory, he

turned in *The Strange Case of Miss Annie Spragg* to a deliberate rejection of material success, and he sought a new kind
of victory based on his instinctive perception of man's ultimate
relationship to the natural order. But this approach was equally
romantic, and it was complicated by a mystic quality that he
could not explain, although he permitted it to dominate the
novel. He was convinced that there was some kind of meaning
inherent in the relationship, but its vagaries forced him to abandon the idea.

At this point, as his fiction between 1929 and 1935 shows,
Bromfield was baffled; having rejected the idea of the triumph
of the natural aristocrat, he continued his preoccupation with
the personal qualities inherent in the type. Consequently, his
fiction of these years is philosophically unresolved as well as
apparently unresolvable. The result is the ambiguous material
and the emotional triumph of the natural aristocrats in *Twenty-
Four Hours* and the complement of that novel, the equally unsatisfactory emotional and material defeat of Pierre Radier in A
Modern Hero. In spite of the excellence of *The Farm* of this
period, Bromfield presents its subject matter as a re-creation of
an ideal that has been destroyed. It can never be revived except
as an impossible nostalgic dream, and the futility of that dream,
or of any dream, is emphasized by the ironic emptiness of *The
Man Who Had Everything*.

The decline of Bromfield's literary reputation began early in
these years, and it was intensified both by the unresolved dilem-
mas of his fiction and by the events in the world around him
which his philosophical floundering forced him to ignore.
Because Bromfield's work during the 1920's had marked him as
one of the period's romantic rebels against modern materialism,
he had been regarded as a young man to watch. But in his
personal dilemma he was not interested in manning the bar-
ricades in the economic crisis of the early 1930's; hence to the
prevailing critical view, led by reviewers in *The Nation* and *The
New Republic,* he had become a reactionary.

But his personal support of the New Deal during its early years
points out that Bromfield was interested in social revolution
rather than in the economic revolution advocated by those
reviewers; he had thought that the historic agrarian bias of the
Democratic Party of his father would lead to a Jeffersonian rejection of materialism and industrialism. Instead, when the New

Deal advanced its program in essentially economic terms within the framework of industrialism and the dehumanized mass society, Bromfield interpreted it as a Hamiltonian and Jacksonian movement designed to aggrandize the state as an impersonal force; and he would have none of it.

Bromfield's eventual rejection of the New Deal emphasizes his belief that somehow, in spite of all the contrary evidence, the Jeffersonian ideal might yet be attainable. His trips to India provided the first tangible evidence to indicate that such a possibility did exist if given the right sort of plan, the dedication and cooperation of the right sort of people, the natural aristocrats on whatever social or economic level one might find them, the cooperation of the state, and the emulation of the order inherent in the natural universe. The transformation and regeneration of Tom Ashford is essentially the story of Bromfield's return to faith in the attainability of the Jeffersonian ideal.

From this point Bromfield's philosophical dilemma had been resolved on the intellectual level, but it still remained for him to translate it into reality and to take into account the coming materialistic Armageddon of World War II. Both major wars of the twentieth century are extremely important in Bromfield's life as well as in his thinking: the first, because it marks the destruction of an ideal; the second, because it makes possible its re-creation. With his return to the farm—convinced that he could realize the Jeffersonian ideal of an agrarian self-sufficiency and freedom in the rolling countryside of Richland County, Ohio—Bromfield suddenly found that writing fiction was no longer important. In fact, because it had brought material success without personal fulfillment, he began to regard it as merely another means of earning a living, and not a particularly satisfying one when compared to the life he had been seeking so long and had finally found.

This attitude produced a number of poor novels and other fiction, notably *Night In Bombay, Wild Is the River, Until the Day Break,* and *What Became of Anna Bolton,* primarily because Bromfield had begun to regard fiction as a utilitarian tool for propaganda rather than as a medium of artistic expression. But the same period produced *Mrs. Parkington* and *The Wild Country,* novels that were almost as good as his best, an indication that Bromfield found much more satisfaction and meaning in writing fiction than his contrary statements imply. However, by this time it was no longer his major interest, for he devoted most of his energy to restoring the soil of "Malabar Farm."

During the years between 1940 and the early 1950's Bromfield came as close to attaining his Jeffersonian ideal as he could, perhaps as near to it as it is possible to come. At "Malabar"—caught up in the cycle of the natural order; learning to understand and emulate its operations as he observed, experimented, and interpreted; applying its lessons to the farm, the country, and the world as he let his thoughts and his writing range widely—he began to see himself as the complete man in the tradition of Jefferson, Franklin, and the other sons of The Enlightenment. Like them, he was unafraid of controversy and confident of his reasoning power; so he disseminated his observations and conclusions widely, making in such works as *Malabar Farm* and *Out of the Earth* substantial contributions to the literature of agriculture and nature. Although experience taught him the futility of his dream of self-sufficiency, it could not lessen the sense of triumph of those years in which he had apparently found the end of his romantic quest.

Nor did the irony of his last months, in which he was forced to commit the cardinal sin of the new agriculture by selling the hilltop forest of "Malabar," or the fact that economics prevented his children from maintaining the farm, make a mockery either of his quest or of how close he came to success. Through the thirty volumes of wide-ranging works that he produced, through the Louis Bromfield Ecological Center at "Malabar," through the continued high rate of circulation his books have in public libraries, and through the countless people who have come to know and love the land through his influence, it is certain that his reason told him his quest had no end—and indeed none is apparent.

In all his works Bromfield is very much a Midwesterner and an agrarian romantic in spite of the veneer of sophistication that overlies so much of his fiction. He belongs properly in the stream of American literature that came out of the Midwest in the first thirty years of the twentieth century and for a while came close to dominating American fiction. In spirit Bromfield is very close to Sherwood Anderson who, like Bromfield, came out of Ohio to seek the meaning of the individual in an industrial age and eventually was forced to withdraw to the Virginia hills where he could come closer to a simple society that materialism had made impossible elsewhere. Bromfield was never the artist that Sherwood Anderson was; and he did not, perhaps could not, create a *Winesburg, Ohio.* But in philosophy, in faith in his fellow man, and in his rejection of the phony and the material superficiality of American life, he was very close in spirit to his fellow Ohioan. Bromfield's quest, like Anderson's, has been largely misinterpreted. But whereas the misinterpretation of Anderson's has led to loose categorization of him as a naturalist rather than as the romantic idealist that he was, Bromfield, condemned as being commercial, has suffered a worse literary fate through the misunderstanding of his work.

In spirit, too, Bromfield is closely related to the Midwestern poets of his time—Vachel Lindsay, Edgar Lee Masters, and Carl Sandburg; but again his artistry suffers when compared to theirs. Like them and like Anderson, he was a romantic who sought to discover what had happened to the dream of the perfect society that had been brought over the mountains from the East almost a hundred years before any of them was born, and had then been lost in the same human frailties of greed, misunderstanding, and puritan morality that had prevented its achievement in the East. As factory smoke contaminated the air and dehumanized the people, Bromfield was one of the many young men who came out of the towns and villages to try to determine why and to seek, if possible, a cure for the malady that was rampant. Of these young men, perhaps Bromfield came closest to finding what he sought.

Bromfield, like the others, might have been more successful in his literary career had he written a hundred years earlier in the age of the great Romantics whose world view was uncluttered by industrialism or economics. But forced to carry on his search in a post-Darwinian world and cognizant of the forces that limit and to a great extent direct the course of human life, he encountered in his fiction the rational roadblocks that made ultimate fulfillment impossible for his people. Invariably, however, he was aware of the importance of dignity and of the human values that led the earlier Romantics to the same kind of fulfillment in defeat that was his own lot.

In many respects Bromfield is also related to the agrarian romantics such as Liberty Hyde Bailey and to the Southern Agrarians led by John Crowe Ransom. Like Bailey, in his later years he constantly extolled the dignity, wisdom, and freedom inherent in the life close to nature; and like the Southern Agrarians, he deplored the dehumanizing influences of modern industry. But, unlike the Agrarians, Bromfield recognized that industry was here to stay and that to bemoan, like Miniver Cheevy, the loss of the old values was futile. Man had to learn to rise above materialism rather than merely to reject it, and this search for a means rather than romantic regret provided the impetus that brought much of his work into being.

To assess Bromfield's contribution to American literature is not difficult: the many shortcomings that had prevented the fulfillment of his early promise are serious enough to keep him out of the first rank of American novelists. But at the same time he deserves a much better literary fate than he has received, because of his effectiveness of style, his character portrayal, and his narrative technique that are his most consistent strong points; because he has made substantial contributions in individual works; and because of his effective and intelligent interpretations of the American scene and American life.

The decline of American individualism and agrarian democracy, the growth of industrialism, the unique role of the strong woman in American society, and the egalitarian nature of a country that permits a young person to rise above his social origins, are themes with which Bromfield dealt significantly and well; in his use of them in his work, he came close to the essence of America as thoughtful Americans know it. That he did not go on to chronicle the rise of an industrial democracy, as has been protested by his major critics and detractors, but attempted instead to return to the past, does not detract from the effectiveness with which he handled these major American themes. Rather it strengthens them as he reiterates the human values on which the country was built rather than the material values with which it asserts world leadership, and he emphasizes the need for those values in a world devoted to things.

Among the substantial literary contributions that he made, one must include the four panel novels, all of which combine to document in human rather than sociological terms the impact upon the individual of sweeping social changes and of perverted values. These novels are valuable, too, because they illustrate Bromfield's narrative talents: a forthright, effective, and literate style; an ability to draw characters that are both human and intense; and a talent for first-rate storytelling—all of which combine into well-constructed, fast-moving novels that are both read-able and believable.

To these novels must be added his best single work, *The Farm; Twenty-Four Hours,* a remarkable *tour de force* of control and intensity in spite of its melodramatic lapses; and *The Rains Came,* certainly the most dramatic as well as the most philo-sophically unified of all his novels. From the last group *Mrs. Parkington* must be included as an intensely human portrait of a magnificent American woman; and *The Wild Country,* too, in which he came close to defining the American Midwestern expe-rience as it reached the peak of one phase of its development and was about to enter another. These, together with a number of short stories—most notably "The Life of Vergie Winters"—com-pose a respectable and substantial body of work in spite of the lapses and failures that marred his career. Were they all he had done, they would have been considerable.

In addition to these achievements one must take into consid-eration Bromfield's contributions to the literature of nature, of folklore, and of agriculture. Most of the best of his folklore and nature writing have been included in *Animals and Other People,* but almost all of it carries universal overtones that place it in the top rank of such writing. This phase of Bromfield's career is certainly the most frequently ignored in spite of the fact that it is a delightful, informative, and important part of his total literary output. Certainly "The Cycle of a Farm Pond" deserves a major place in the history of romantic nature writing, and such essays as "My Ninety Acres" and the others in which he probes the close kinship between past and present, man and nature, are examples of what the modern re-creation of folk legend can be but so seldom is.

Finally, and perhaps most importantly, Bromfield must be regarded as important for his contributions to the field of agri-culture and to its literature, a field of activity that for too long has been dominated by the charts and graphs of profit-loss ratios that ignore love and respect for the land and the soil. Assess-ment of his specific contributions to agricultural theory and prac-tice is beyond the province of the literary historian and critic; and perhaps it is difficult for the agricultural scientist without the further verification and experimentation that scientific judg-ment demands. As literature, however, his agricultural writings are significant because they occupy such a prominent place in the Bromfield canon and because they provide clear-cut examples of the philosophy of The Enlightenment. That philosophy is modified by the impacts of romanticism and of Darwinism, but nevertheless it is recognizable as the logical intellectual descendant of that great tradition. The spirit of The Enlightenment has largely disappeared under the assault of material philosophies, but Bromfield provides valuable insight into its meaning and continuance. Furthermore, these agricultural writings are for the most part examples of what technical writing can be when it is lucid, free of jargon and unnecessary scientific terminology, and written with an imagination and insight that give it life. Much of it is a permanent and valuable addition to the literature of science.

These, then, are the contributions that Bromfield has made to American literature. While they are not enough to justify a high place in the history of that literature and while it is easy to protest that he might have contributed a great deal more, protests and their implied or actual denunciations are futile. Bromfield was what he was: a man plagued by a personal philosophical dilemma that could not be resolved or removed through literature; and he was forced to look elsewhere for a solution. Such a fate has been common to writers in the mainstream of American literature from Herman Melville to John Steinbeck, and perhaps Bromfield was more fortunate than most in the effects of the search beyond literature; certainly he achieved a sense of fulfillment and justification that has eluded a great many writers considered to be more significant than he, and at the same time he also contributed to agriculture, a field vital to America and the world. Perhaps if the world can learn to feed itself and to live in peace—as Bromfield asserted could be done and as he attempted to prove—his place in history will indeed be high.

Unfortunately, however, current critical consensus relegates Bromfield to a much lower place in American literary history than his accomplishments deserve, primarily because he, like so many others, has suffered from the lack of objective criticism. The unjust stereotypes that emerged in the early 1930's and persist to the present among many serious critics have for too long prevented a clear, coherent look at his work. Yet the weaknesses of these stereotyped views are obvious: commercial success does not preclude literary merit; and, adversely, criticism that results from political or economic differences reveals an inability or an unwillingness to assess a work for what it is rather than for what one would have it say. The dispersion of these myths so that the works themselves may be seen for what they are is essential to their adequate assessment.

In his accomplishments and his failures Bromfield epitomizes much that is wrong and much that is right in twentieth-century American writing. He provides a graphic example of a man who could and did write too well too easily, thus making it easy to comply with the demands of publisher and public, both of whom were insatiable for his work. He illustrates, too, the adverse effects of early commercial and critical success, both of which, while pleasing to the young writer, force him to live under the shadow of demands that not even an old professional can resist.

Most of all, Bromfield represents the typically American problem that results from the inability to reconcile the American dream with the American reality. Bromfield's commercial success enabled him to avoid the usual unpleasant results of that problem because it permitted him to escape into new areas of concentration that would absorb his romantic energy and insight; in this respect, he was far more fortunate than most American writers. But the problem is evident in the works of serious writers from Sherwood Anderson to the post-World War II group, all of whom sought futilely to transcend the gap between the world as it is and the world as they would have liked it to be.

In the final analysis Bromfield is worth reading today if only because he was willing to meet most of the major problems of his era head-on in his fiction and at the same time to attempt to explain or resolve them in terms that are at once romantic and rational. His approaches to solutions are certainly questionable in many respects, but his refusal to take refuge in easy solutions or pat answers in response to his critics is commendable. But, more importantly, Bromfield is worth reading because at his best he was very good, because he told a good story well, because he had the gift of constructing characters that are both believable and memorable; and because he was the master rather than the servant of the words that form the basis of his craft. These are not common abilities in any literary age.

Notes and References

Chapter One

1. All biographical information, unless otherwise cited, comes from Morrison Brown, *Louis Bromfield and His Books* (Fair Lawn, N.J., 1957); Ellen Bromfield Geld, *The Heritage, a Daughter's Memories of Louis Bromfield* (New York, 1962); Louis Bromfield, *The Farm* (New York, 1934); and from conversations with Mr. Bromfield.

Chapter Two

1. Louis Bromfield, *The Green Bay Tree* (New York, 1924), p. 107.
2. *Ibid.*, p. 341.
3. Louis Bromfield, Foreword to *Possession* (New York, 1925).
4. *Ibid.*, p. 80.
5. Louis Bromfield, *A Good Woman* (New York, 1927), p. 14.
6. *Ibid.*, p. 75.

Chapter Three

1. Mary Bromfield, "The Writer I Live With," *The Atlantic Monthly*, CLXXXVI (August, 1950), 78.
2. Gertrude Stein, *The Autobiography of Alice B. Toklas* (New York, 1933), pp. 305-6.
3. Ellen Bromfield Geld, *The Heritage*, p. 156.
4. Louis Bromfield, *Twenty-Four Hours* (New York, 1930), p. 398.
5. Henry Seidel Canby, "America Concentrated," *The Saturday Review of Literature*, VII (September 20, 1930), 137.
6. Eugene Löhrke, "Satirist-and Victim," *The Nation, CXXXI* November 5, 1930), 503.
7. Bromfield, *Twenty-Four Hours*, p. 246.
8. Percy Hutchinson, "Mr. Bromfield's Story of a Philanderer," New York *Times Book Review*, IV (May 1, 1932), 6.
9. Clifton Fadiman, "A Modern Novelist," *The Nation*, CXXXV (July 13, 1932), 40.
10. Louis Bromfield, dedication of *A Modern Hero* (New York, 1932).

Chapter Four

1. Louis Bromfield, *The Farm* (New York, 1934), p. 177.
2. *Ibid.*, p. 224.
3. *Ibid.*, p. 225.
4. *Ibid.*, p. 147.
5. Erskine Caldwell, "Brilliant and Tedious," *The Nation,* CXXXVII (September 6, 1933), 277.
6. Louis Bromfield, *The Man Who Had Everything* (New York, 1935), pp. 51-52.

Chapter Five

1. Louis Bromfield, headnote to selection from *The Rains Came* in *This Is My Best*, ed. by Whit Burnett (New York, 1942), p. 913.
2. Louis Bromfield, *Night In Bombay* (New York, 1940), p. 13.
3. *Ibid.*, p. 238.

Chapter Six

1. Louis Bromfield, *Until the Day Break* (New York, 1942), p. 51.

Chapter Seven

1. Ellen Bromfield Geld, *The Heritage*, p. 153.
2. Louis Bromfield, *Out of the Earth* (New York, 1950), p. 298.
3. Louis Bromfield, *Animals and Other People* (New York, 1955), p. xii.
4. *Ibid.*, p. xi.

Selected Bibliography

PRIMARY SOURCES

1. Books by Louis Bromfield (listed chronologically)

   The Green Bay Tree. New York: Frederick A. Stokes, 1924.
   Possession. New York: Frederick A. Stokes, 1925.
   Early Autumn. New York: Frederick A. Stokes, 1926.
   A Good Woman. New York: Frederick A. Stokes, 1927.
   The Strange Case of Miss Annie Spragg. New York: Frederick A. Stokes, 1928.
   Awake and Rehearse. New York: Frederick A. Stokes, 1929.
   Twenty-Four Hours. New York: Frederick A. Stokes, 1930.
   A Modern Hero. New York: Frederick A. Stokes, 1932.
   The Farm. New York: Harper and Brothers, 1934.
   Here Today and Gone Tomorrow. New York: Harper and Brothers, 1934.
   The Man Who Had Everything. New York: Harper and Brothers, 1935.
   The Rains Came. New York: Harper and Brothers, 1937.
   It Takes All Kinds. New York: Harper and Brothers, 1939.
   Night In Bombay. New York: Harper and Brothers, 1940.
   Wild Is the River. New York: Harper and Brothers, 1941.
   Until the Day Break. New York: Harper and Brothers, 1942.
   Mrs. Parkington. New York: Harper and Brothers, 1943.
   The World We Live In. New York: Harper and Brothers, 1944.
   What Became of Anna Bolton. New York: Harper and Brothers, 1944.
   Pleasant Valley. New York: Harper and Brothers, 1945.
   A Few Brass Tacks. New York: Harper and Brothers, 1946.
   Kenny. New York: Harper and Brothers, 1947.
   Colorado. New York: Harper and Brothers, 1947.
   Malabar Farm. New York: Harper and Brothers, 1948.
   The Wild Country. New York: Harper and Brothers, 1948.
   Out of the Earth. New York: Harper and Brothers, 1950.
   Mr. Smith. New York: Harper and Brothers, 1951.
   A New Pattern for a Tired World. New York: Harper and Brothers, 1954.

From My Experience. New York: Harper and Brothers, 1955.
Animals and Other People. New York: Harper and Brothers, 1955.

2. Chapters of Books

In *Bobbed Hair,* by twenty authors. New York: Putman, 1925.
"Expatriate—Vintage 1927," *Mirrors of the Year 1926-27.* Ed. by Grant Overton. New York: Frederick A. Stokes, 1927.
"A Critique of Criticism," *Mirrors of the Year 1927-28.* Ed. by Horace Winston Stokes. New York: Frederick A. Stokes, 1928.
"The Novel in Transition," *Revolt in the Arts.* Ed. by Oliver Martin Sayler. New York: Brentano's, 1930.
"Hawthorne," *The Writers of American Literature.* Ed. by John Macy. New York: Horace Liveright, 1931.
"To Clear the Dross," *Cities Are Abnormal.* Ed. by Elmer T. Peterson. Norman: University of Oklahoma Press, 1946.
"Introduction to The Midwest," *Look at the U.S.A.* Ed. of *Look.* Boston: Houghton Mifflin, 1947.

3. Miscellaneous Uncollected Pieces

"We Are Not in Georgia" (short story), *Good Housekeeping,* CXII (January, 1941).
"Crime Passionel" (short story), *The New Yorker,* XX (March 25, 1944).
"Les Demoiselles" (short story), *The New Yorker,* XXI (May 26, 1945).
"Reflexions Sur le Capitalisme Americain," Aujourd'hui (September 24, 1931). Contains comments on the nature of capitalism in America.
"England Is Herself Again," *The Daily Telegraph,* London (December 30, 1931). Contains an appreciation of England's recovery from the war and from the economic difficulties of the 1920's.
"Gertrude Stein, Experimenter with Words," New York *Herald Tribune Books* (September 3, 1933). Comments primarily on Stein's personality.
"A Very Strange Flirtation," *The Daily Herald,* London (August 25, 1936). Castigates those who ignore or profit from Hitler's rise to power.

"Rebirth of An American Farm," *Reader's Digest*, XLIII (September, 1943). Recounts the early successes at "Malabar."

SECONDARY SOURCES

1. Books

BROWN, MORRISON. *Louis Bromfield and His Books*. Fair Lawn, N.J.: Essential Books, 1957. Primarily a biographical apology.

GELD, ELLEN BROMFIELD. *The Heritage, a Daughter's Memories of Louis Bromfield*. New York: Harper and Brothers, 1962. A delightful, remarkably acute biographical memoir.

2. Essays, Reviews, and Sections of Books

BROMFIELD, MARY. "The Writer I Live With," *The Atlantic Monthly*, CLXXVI (August, 1950). Recounts Bromfield's life and experiences.

CALDWELL, ERSKINE. "Brilliant and Tedious," *The Nation*, CXXXVII (September 6, 1933). A generally weak review of *The Farm*.

CANBY, HENRY SEIDEL. "America Concentrated," *The Saturday Review of Literature*, VII (September 20, 1930). A generally favorable review of *Twenty-Four Hours*.

CARGILL, OSCAR. *Intellectual America*. New York: Macmillan, 1948. Illustrates clearly the emergence of critical contempt.

CARTER, JOHN. "A Middle Western Factory Town," *The New York Times Book Review* (March 30, 1924). A favorable review of *The Green Bay Tree*.

COMMAGER, HENRY STEELE. "Louis Bromfield Looks Backward," *The Saturday Review of Literature*, IX (August 19, 1933). Comments favorably on Bromfield's career and on *The Farm*.

FADIMAN, CLIFTON. "A Modern Novelist," *The Nation*, CXXXV (July 13, 1932). A review of *A Modern Hero* that typifies the kind of adverse criticism leveled by the liberal journals.

HUTCHINSON, PERCY. "Mr. Bromfield's Story of a Philanderer," *The New York Times Book Review*, IV (May 1, 1932). Approves of *A Modern Hero*.

LÖHRKE, EUGENE. "Satirist—and Victim," *The Nation*, CXXXI November 5, 1930). Commences the attack on Bromfield's "commercialism."

LORD, RUSSELL. "Afterword," in Louis Bromfield, *The Farm.* New York: New American Library, 1961. A personal memoir that emphasizes Bromfield's later years.

MARBLE, ANNIE RUSSELL. "Louis Bromfield," *A Study of the Modern Novel.* New York: Appleton, 1928. Shows the early favorable view, a sharp contrast to Cargill.

Review of *Here Today and Gone Tomorrow, The Nation,* CXXXVII (April 25, 1934). Shows the further deterioration of Bromfield's reputation.

SMITH, HARRISON. "Babbitt of a New Generation," *The Saturday Review of Literature* (August 25, 1951). A favorable review of *Mr. Smith.*

STEIN, GERTRUDE. *The Autobiography of Alice B. Toklas.* New York: Harcourt Brace, 1933. Describes her acquaintance with Bromfield.

WHITE, E. B. Review of *Malabar Farm, The New Yorker,* XXIV (May, 8, 1948). An amusing, favorable review in verse.

WILSON, EDMUND. "What Became of Louis Bromfield," *The New Yorker,* XX (April 1, 1944). A devastating review of *What Became of Anna Bolton.*

3. Bibliography

DERRENBACHER, MERLE. "Louis Bromfield: a Bibliography," *Bulletin of Bibliography,* Vol. XVII, No. 6 (September-December, 1941) and Vol. XVII, No. 7 (January-April, 1942). Primarily valuable for pointing out the variety of general articles about Bromfield and the paucity of serious criticism.

Index

(References to Bromfield's works will be found under the author's name.)

77-98; rejects pragmatism, 88; trips to India, 89; his critics, 89, 92, 110; the plays, 92f.; search for identity and fulfillment, 93; characterizations, 96; the meaningful present, 99-121; on relationship between characters and setting, 102; the return to Ohio, 111-12; opposes attempts to appease Hitler, 111; speeches about European crisis, 112; his most successful portrait of evil personified, 119; the decline of a novelist, 122-50; "Malabar Farm," 127 (*See also* main entry, "Malabar Farm"); attitude toward New and Fair Deals, 135, 156, 165, 173f.; accused of being a reactionary, 135, 158; magazine articles, 136; farming becomes dominant interest, 141, 144; end of career as writer of fiction, 141; pessimism, 149, 150; a cubic foot of soil, 151-70; nonfiction between 1945-1955, 151ff.; major change in direction, 151; compared with Thoreau, 154; alliance with political forces of the economic right, 156; radical departure from the Right, 157, 158, 166; agricultural experience and theories tested outside of Ohio, 161; personal life begins to disintegrate, 161; cure for world's ills, 164; economic and political outlook, 165f.; appraisal of his life, 167; becomes the complete man, 168; as a nature writer, 169; death, 170; in retrospect, 171-80; unity behind apparently different careers, 171; writings the record of a consistent romantic search, 171; two Louis Bromfields? 171; recognizes futility of attempt to escape, 172; decline of literary reputation, 173; interested in social rather than economic revolution, 173; effects of World War I and II, 174; a Midwesterner and agrarian romantic,

175f.; compared with Sherwood Anderson, 175; major American themes, 177; contribution to American literature, 177ff.; current critical consensus, 179; epitomizes much of rights and wrongs of 20th-century American writing, 180; inability to reconcile American dream with American reality, 180; worth reading today, 180

COLORBLIND: A STORY OF RACISM

© 2019 Zuiker Press

Johnathan Harris Photographs © 2019 Johnathan Harris

Written by Anthony E. Zuiker
Art by Donald Hudson
Cover art by Garry Leach
Colors by Fahriza Kamaputra
Lettering by Tyler Smith for Comicraft
Designed by Roberta Melzl
Edited by Dave Elliott

Founders: Michelle & Anthony E. Zuiker
Publisher: David Wilk

Published by Zuiker Press
16255 Ventura Blvd.
Suite #900
Encino, CA 91436
United States of America

Visit us online at www.zuikerpress.com

ISBN 978-1-947378-12-4 (hardcover)

PRINTED IN CANADA
April 2019
10 9 8 7 6 5 4 3 2 1

DEDICATED TO ... every young person who needs to be reminded they are not alone.

HOPE lies within these pages.

ZUIKER PRESS

... is a husband and wife publishing company that champions the voices of young authors. We are an **ISSUE-BASED** literary house. All of our authors have elected to tell their personal stories and be ambassadors of their cause. Their goal, as is ours, is that young people will learn from their pain and heroics and find **HOPE**, **CHANGE**, and **HAPPINESS** in their own lives.

TEACHER'S CORNER

SHANNON LIVELY

is a National Board Certified educator with a bachelor's degree in elementary education from the University of Nevada, Las Vegas, a master's degree from Southern Utah University, as well as advanced degrees in differentiated instruction and technology. In 2013, she was awarded the Barrick Gold One Classroom at a Time grant, and then chosen as Teacher of the Year. She is currently teaching fifth grade at John C. Vanderburg Elementary School in Henderson, Nevada.

WHY WE HONOR TEACHERS

We understand the amount of hard work, time and preparation it takes to be a teacher! At Zuiker Press, we have done the preparation for you. With each book we publish, we have created printable resources for you and your students. Our differentiated reading guides, vocabulary activities, writing prompts, extension activities, assessments, and answer keys are all available in one convenient location. Visit Zuikerpress.com, click on the For Educators tab, and access the **DOWNLOADABLE GUIDES** for teachers. These PDFs include everything you need to print and go! Each lesson is designed to cover Common Core standards for many subjects across the curriculum. We hope these resources help teachers utilize each story to the fullest extent!

12

TWO OF THE MOST IMPORTANT MEN IN MY LIFE... LIVING TWO COMPLETELY DIFFERENT LIVES.

BUT AS DISTANT AND DIVERSE AS THOSE PATHS ARE...

...ROADS SOMEHOW HAVE A WAY OF CROSSING... FINDING EACH OTHER... AND IN THE END...

...IT WOULD LEAD ME DOWN THE ROAD TO SALVATION.

THE FIRST TIME I MET MY UNCLE, HE WAS BEHIND BARS.

I WAS JUST SIX MONTHS OLD.

"THERE IS NO EASY WALK TO FREEDOM ANYWHERE, AND MANY OF US WILL HAVE TO PASS THROUGH THE VALLEY OF THE SHADOW OF DEATH AGAIN AND AGAIN BEFORE WE REACH THE MOUNTAINTOP OF OUR DESIRES."
-NELSON MANDELA

CLEARLY, UNCLE RUSSELL HELPING ME THROUGH LIFE WAS HIS DESIRE.

19

WHAT I DIDN'T KNOW UNTIL MUCH LATER...

...IS THAT MY DESIRE TO LIVE MY LIFE UNDER HIS GUIDANCE WOULD ULTIMATELY BRING US CLOSER TOGETHER...

BUT WE BOTH HAD TO WALK THROUGH SOME TOUGH VALLEYS FIRST... AGAIN AND AGAIN.

21

WHEN I WENT BACK TO SCHOOL, THE OTHER KIDS ASKED WHAT I GOT FOR CHRISTMAS. I TOLD THEM "A GRAY CAR."

WHAT KIND OF GRAY CAR?

MUSTANG?

A PORSCHE?

A FERRARI?

A CAMARO.

BACK THEN, I DIDN'T UNDERSTAND WHAT EXACTLY IT WAS UNCLE RUSSELL WAS TRYING TO TEACH ME.

24

"YELLOW MY FELLOW IS FOR YOUR FELLOW BROS...DON'T THINK THEY HAVEN'T FELT MOST OF YOUR WOES."

"LEARN FROM THEIR ANGER. LEARN FROM THEIR FALLS. YELLOW IS 'HELLO' FOR BREAKIN' DOWN WALLS."

"GREEN IS FOR THE POPS WHO WORKS WITH THE COPS. PROTECTING OUR OWN, SO THEY DON'T END UP HERE. GUESS THAT MAKES HIM MY MAN OF THE YEAR."

"POPS IS GENUINE. POPS IS RIGHT. EVERY TIME YOU SEE HIM, HOLD HIM REAL TIGHT..."

28

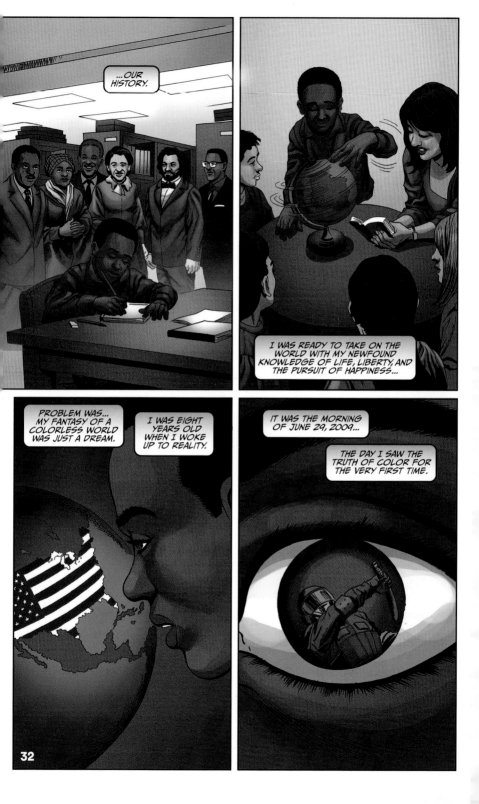

...OUR HISTORY.

I WAS READY TO TAKE ON THE WORLD WITH MY NEWFOUND KNOWLEDGE OF LIFE, LIBERTY, AND THE PURSUIT OF HAPPINESS...

PROBLEM WAS... MY FANTASY OF A COLORLESS WORLD WAS JUST A DREAM.

I WAS EIGHT YEARS OLD WHEN I WOKE UP TO REALITY.

IT WAS THE MORNING OF JUNE 29, 2009...

THE DAY I SAW THE TRUTH OF COLOR FOR THE VERY FIRST TIME.

IT WAS SIX O'CLOCK IN THE MORNING. I HEARD A LOUD BANG ON THE DOOR.

I LOOKED OUTSIDE MY BEDROOM WINDOW AND SAW AN ARMY OF COPS...

POLICE

POLICE

SWAT WITH SHOTGUNS AND SHIELDS.

GO! GO! GO!!

SWAT BARRELED THROUGH OUR FRONT DOOR AND INVADED OUR HOUSE LIKE ANGRY FIRE ANTS.

33

35

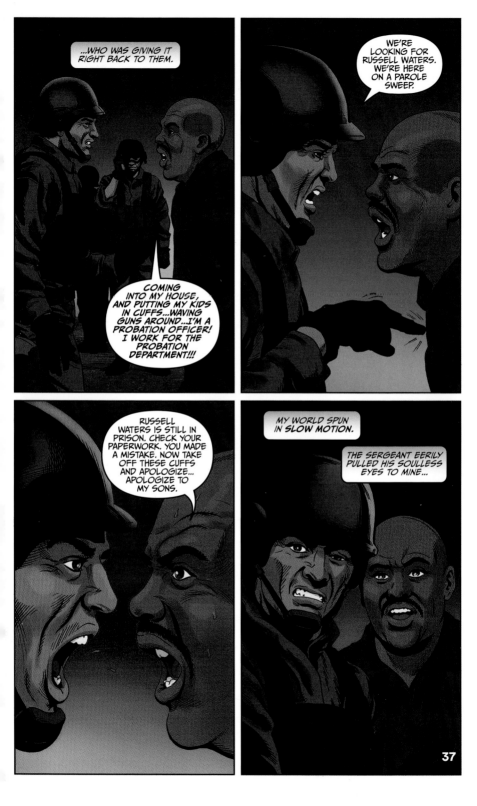

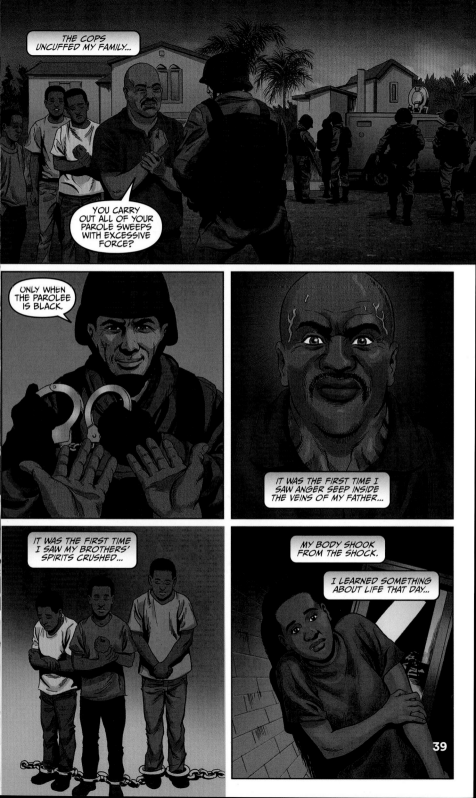

THE COPS UNCUFFED MY FAMILY...

YOU CARRY OUT ALL OF YOUR PAROLE SWEEPS WITH EXCESSIVE FORCE?

ONLY WHEN THE PAROLEE IS BLACK.

IT WAS THE FIRST TIME I SAW ANGER SEEP INSIDE THE VEINS OF MY FATHER...

IT WAS THE FIRST TIME I SAW MY BROTHERS' SPIRITS CRUSHED...

MY BODY SHOOK FROM THE SHOCK.

I LEARNED SOMETHING ABOUT LIFE THAT DAY...

39

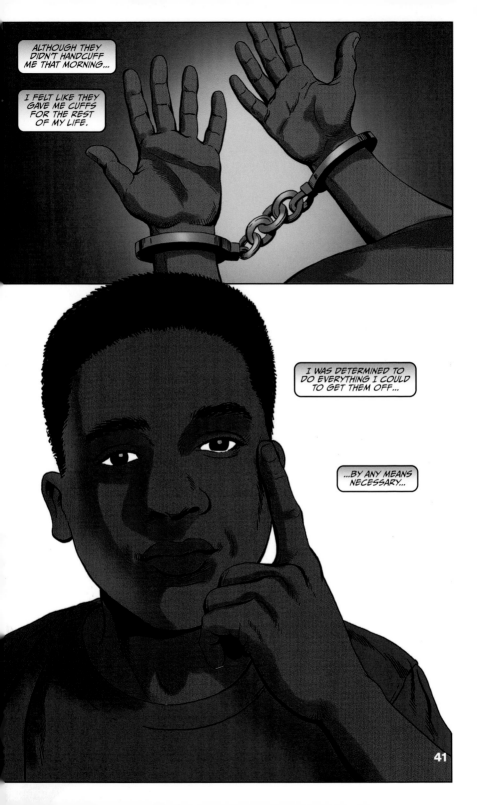

41

LAST THING MY MOM WANTED WAS A SON GROWING UP IN THE WORLD ANGRY AND BITTER.

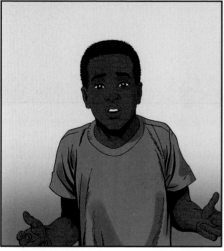

MOM WASN'T HAVING IT...

42

MY UNCLE RUSSELL WAS FOUR HOURS AWAY BY CAR...

I WAS ON MY OWN WITH THIS ONE. I ONLY HAD TWO CHOICES...

...PLAY OR QUIT.

AND I'VE NEVER QUIT ANYTHING IN MY LIFE...

47

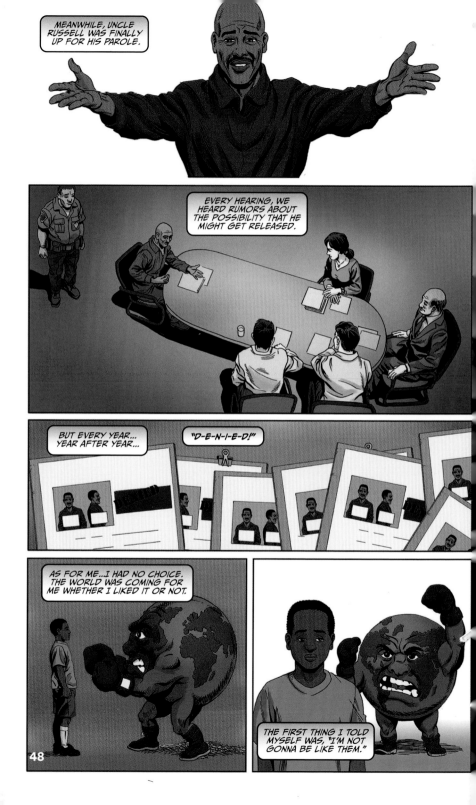

MY MOM AND DAD WOULD TRY TO EXPLAIN HOW "THE LORD WORKS IN MYSTERIOUS WAYS."

BUT MYSTERIOUS WAYS DON'T HELP A CHILD IN NEED OF ANSWERS.

I WAS ALONE... IN UNCHARTED WATERS...

49

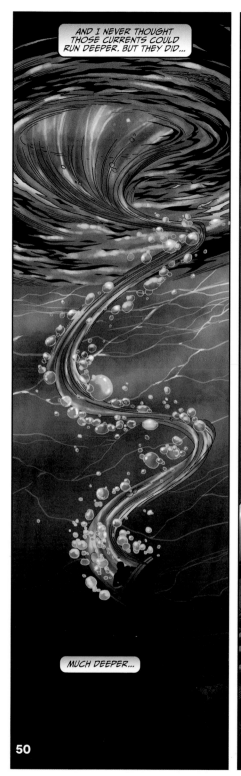

50

SOON AFTER, I JOINED THE BOY SCOUTS TO LEARN ABOUT SURVIVAL. BETWEEN SOCCER, SCHOOL, AND THE STREETS, "SURVIVAL" WAS MY MIDDLE NAME.

THAT SUMMER, OUR TROOP WENT ON A FIELD TRIP TO THE SHERIFF'S DEPARTMENT TO SEE REAL COPS IN ACTION.

AS WE FILED OUT FROM THE MEMORIAL WALL TO THE MAIN LOBBY...

I SAW HIM IN THE ELEVATOR.

THAT SAME SERGEANT FROM THE NIGHT THE COPS RAIDED OUR HOUSE.

MY BLOOD RAN COLD. TIME STOOD STILL.

51

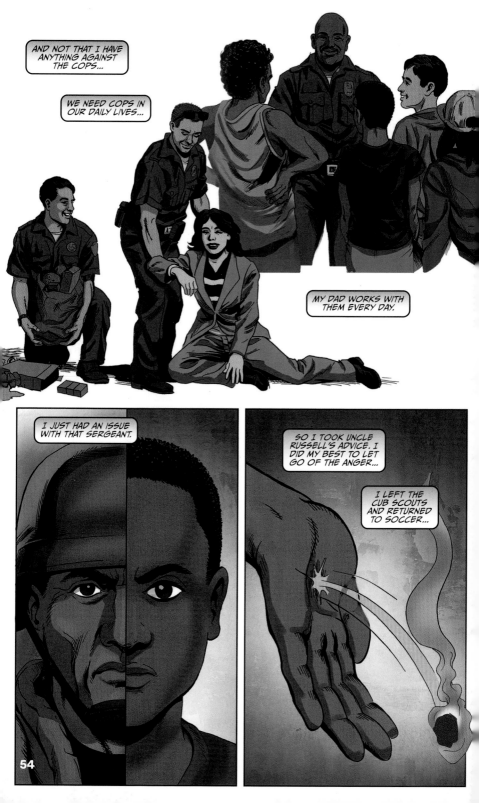

56

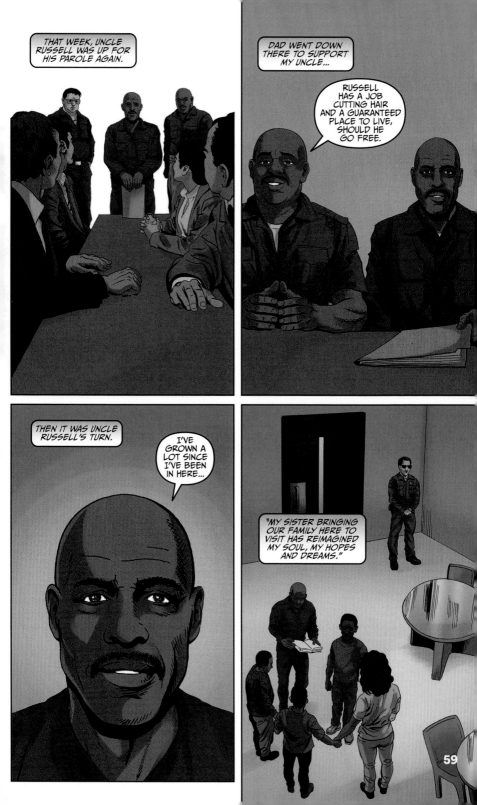

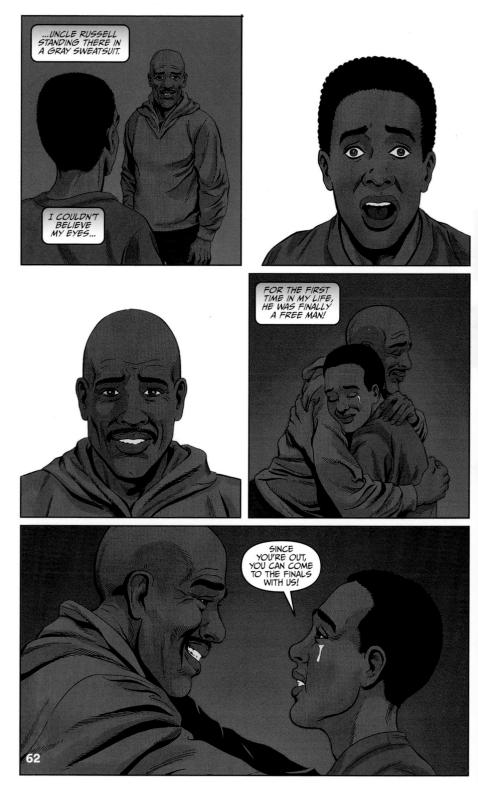

63

65

I WON IN HERE. THE HEART...

EPILOGUE:
WHERE AM I NOW?

TODAY, I AM GOING INTO THE 11TH GRADE. A JUNIOR IN HIGH SCHOOL.

I'M STUDYING HARD, GETTING GOOD GRADES, AND FOCUSING ON MY FUTURE.

I'M PLAYING VARSITY FOOTBALL. I'M A KICKER!

LAST YEAR, I BOOTED A 50-YARD FIELD GOAL AND HELPED MY TEAM WIN.

MY DREAM IS TO PLAY FOOTBALL FOR UCLA, WHERE I HOPE TO GO AFTER I GRADUATE.

WHO KNOWS IF I'LL GET THE OPPORTUNITY TO PLAY IN THE NFL...

I JUST WANT TO PURSUE A CAREER IN HELPING YOUNG PEOPLE.

I PLAN TO BECOME A REGISTERED NURSE.

75

I THINK DR. KING WOULDN'T MIND ME RIFFING OFF HIS WORDS...

FOR IT IS THIS "COLORBLIND" WORLD I LIVE IN THAT ALLOWS ME NOW...

...AND DR. KING THEN...

...TO TRULY BE FREE.

76

NEVER THE END...

ABOUT OUR AUTHOR

JOHNATHAN HARRIS is an African American teenager from Long Beach, California. He is the youngest of four brothers in a close-knit family. His father is a deputy probation officer, and his mother is a registered nurse. He loves to play competitive soccer, tackle football, and is an ardent fan of rap music, especially Snoop Dogg, Long Beach's native son. Johnathan hopes that his story about overcoming racism will help others to see multi-culturalism in our society, not color.

JOHNATHAN...

Artwork from kindergarten. I wanted to be a police officer like my dad.

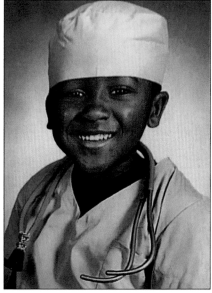

Did anyone call a nurse? I'm here . . .

Just floating through life at 3-years-old. Me, on our yearly trip to Palm Springs.

78

JOHNATHAN...

This is a picture of my mom, dad, and brother visiting Uncle Russell in prison.

This is the State Cup when I played for FC Long Beach.

My brothers and me. I'm obviously the ham.

JOHNATHAN...

This is me in front of the famous VIP Records in Long Beach, CA.

Mr. Pete's Burgers. This is where Uncle Russell surprised me. A free man at last!

Uncle Russell and me in his barber shop. He charges everyone only five dollars.

This is my one big happy family . . . anchored by my Great Grandma.

TAKE 5!

FIVE PARENT TAKE-AWAYS ABOUT RACISM

ROBERT W. CLARK

Robert W. Clark is a Former Senior FBI Official who served as the Assistant Special Agent in Charge for the city of Los Angeles. After a 30-year career, Mr. Clark oversaw various criminal programs for the FBI, including the Gang and Violent Crime Units.

CULTURE, NOT SKIN COLOR, MATTERS MOST.

America is a melting pot of cultures. It's what makes our country so great. In order to truly honor each other, we must embrace and take a genuine interest in our various backgrounds. Our differences provide the foundation upon which every man, woman, and child can be equal.

THERE ARE GOOD COPS AND BAD COPS, BUT MOSTLY GREAT COPS.

Law enforcement is a tough job. It is not until you walk in the shoes of a police officer that you can truly understand the complexity and dangers involved in keeping civilians safe. In my 30-year career, I've found one immutable truth: Most people in law enforcement are great at what they do. It's not a money job. It's a calling and passion for service.

IF YOU DO NOT WANT YOUR KIDS TO GROW UP ANGRY, LISTEN WITH A KIND AND PATIENT HEART.

It's no secret racism still plays a significant role in our country. Parents, speak with your children about their daily lives. If something hurts their feelings, listen and teach them to "lead with patient love" and to find effective ways of dealing with the world.

SOCIAL MEDIA IS WHERE A LOT OF FIRES START.

We all know the big three social media sites. For parents, my strong suggestion is that you know the passwords and monitor what your children are consuming and serving on social media. Be "friends" with them on social media so you can be engaged in what they are posting. Young people are more apt to lash out online as a cry for help or to vent justified frustration. This is your cue to put out the fire by speaking one-on-one with your child, and providing other supportive services.

REACQUAINT YOURSELF WITH THE WORKS OF MARTIN LUTHER KING, NELSON MANDELA, AND MAYA ANGELOU.

We grew up consuming iconic works/ orations, such as "I Have A Dream" (MLK), Long Walk to Freedom (Mandela), and I Know Why the Caged Bird Sings (Angelou). Read these with your children. It's important for young people, especially young African American boys and girls, to understand how these pillars of truth have made positive changes for every race, creed, and color.

THE STORY DOESN'T END HERE...

VISIT
ZUIKERPRESS.COM

... to learn more about Johnathan's story, see behind-the-scenes videos of Johnathan and his family, and learn more about how to overcome **RACISM**.

Our **WEBSITE** is another resource to help our readers deal with the issues that they face every day. Log on to find advice from experts, links to helpful organizations and literature, and more real-life experiences from young people just like you.

Spotlighting young writers with heartfelt stories that enlighten and inspire.

ABOUT OUR
FOUNDERS

MICHELLE ZUIKER is a retired educator who taught 2nd through 4th grade for seventeen years. Mrs. Zuiker spent most of her teaching years at Blue Ribbon school John C. Vanderburg Elementary School in Henderson, Nevada.

ANTHONY E. ZUIKER is the creator and Executive Producer of the hit CSI television franchise, *CSI: Crime Scene Investigation (Las Vegas)*, *CSI: Miami*, *CSI: New York*, and *CSI: Cyber* on CBS. Mr. Zuiker resides in Los Angeles with his wife and three sons.

ABOUT OUR ILLUSTRATORS & EDITOR...

DON HUDSON– ILLUSTRATOR

Don Hudson has been a professional artist in Los Angeles for twenty years. He's had the opportunity to work in comics, animation, advertising and even Broadway!

If you want to know more about Don, go to **www.dchudson.blogspot.com**.

GARRY LEACH– COVER ARTIST

is a British artist best known for his work co-creating the new *Marvelman* with writer Alan Moore. As an artist Garry was a frequent contributor to *2000AD* working on *Dan Dare*, *Judge Dredd*, *The V.C.s.* and *Future Shocks*. At DC Comics Garry worked on *Legion of Superheroes*, *Hit Man*, *Monarchy* and *Global Frequency,* while over at Marvel Comics, he inked Chris Weston on *The Twelve*. Garry has been a cover artist for Marvel, DC, *2000AD*, *Eclipse*, *Dynamic Forces*, and Kellogg's Corn Flakes.

FAHRIZA KAMAPUTRA–COLORIST

was born and raised in southern Jakarta. In 2010 he worked as colorist on a local comic book, *Vienetta and the Stupid Aliens,* which led to his work on the web comic *Rokki,* and Madeleine Holly-Rosling's *Boston Metaphysical Society* with the studio STELLAR LABS. Fahriza now works as a freelance artist.

DAVE ELLIOTT–EDITOR

has more than thirty-five years of experience working and garnering awards in every aspect of the entertainment industry, from writer and artist, to editor and publisher. Dave has worked on diverse titles such as *A1, Deadline, Viz Comic, Heavy Metal* magazine, *2000AD, Justice League of America, Transformers, GI Joe,* the *Real Ghostbusters* and *Doctor Who*. He also developed projects for Johnny Depp, Dwayne Johnson, and Tom Cruise. Through his own company, AtomekArt, Dave has created his own graphic novel series, *Odyssey* and *The Weirding Willows*.

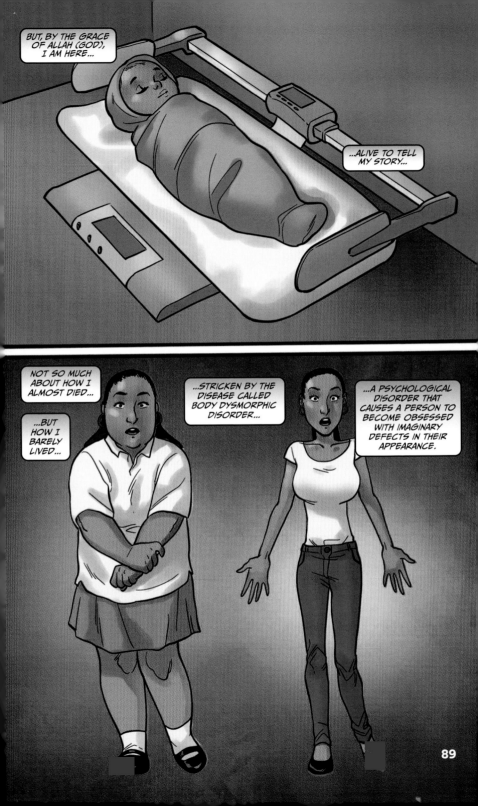

NEW FOR SPRING 2019

IMPERFECT: A STORY OF BODY IMAGE

COLORBLIND: A STORY OF RACISM

COMING FALL 2019

ACTIVIST: A STORY OF THE MARJORY STONEMAN DOUGLAS SHOOTING

IDENTITY: A STORY OF TRANSITIONING